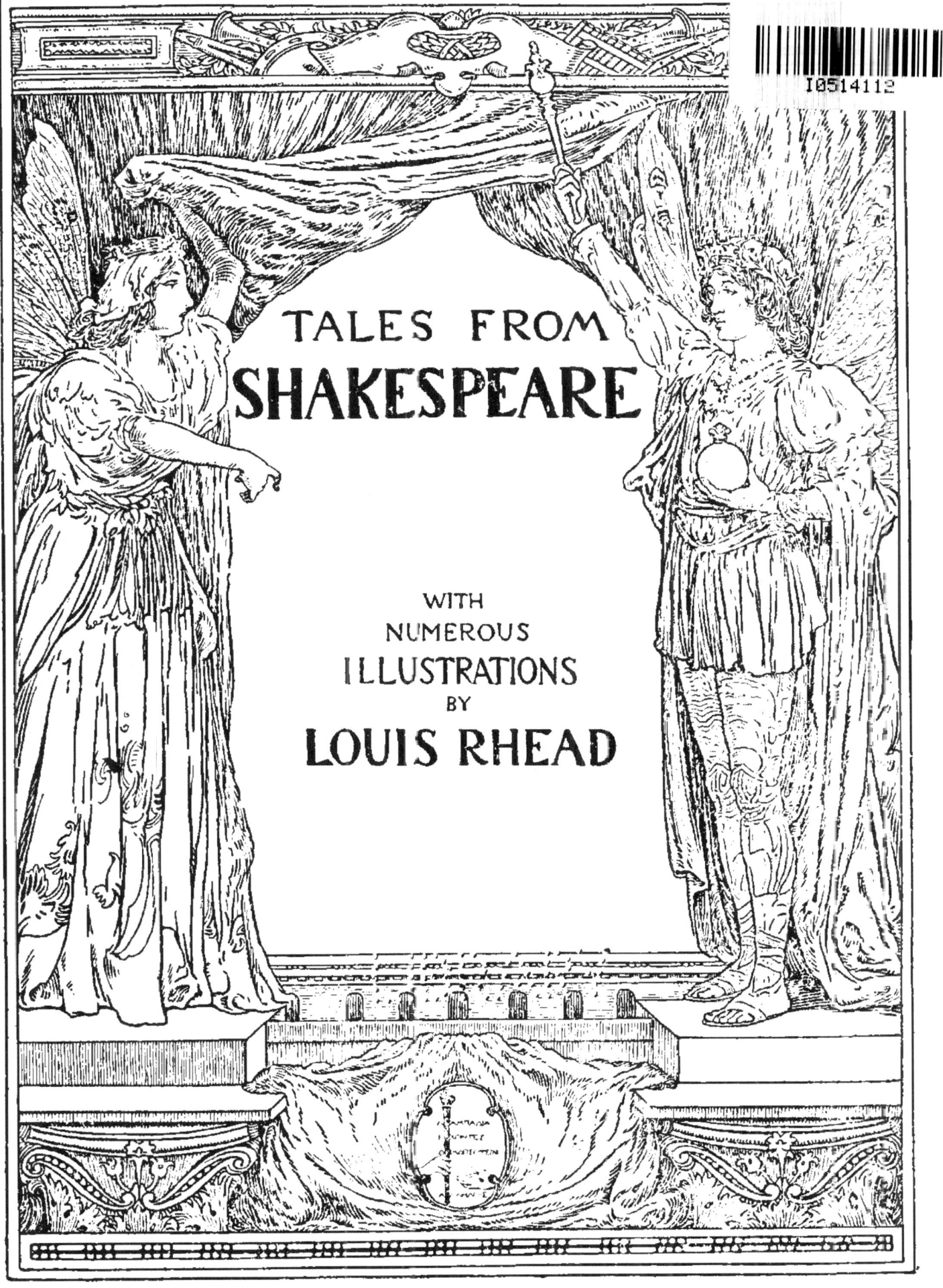

TALES FROM SHAKESPEARE

WITH NUMEROUS ILLUSTRATIONS BY LOUIS RHEAD

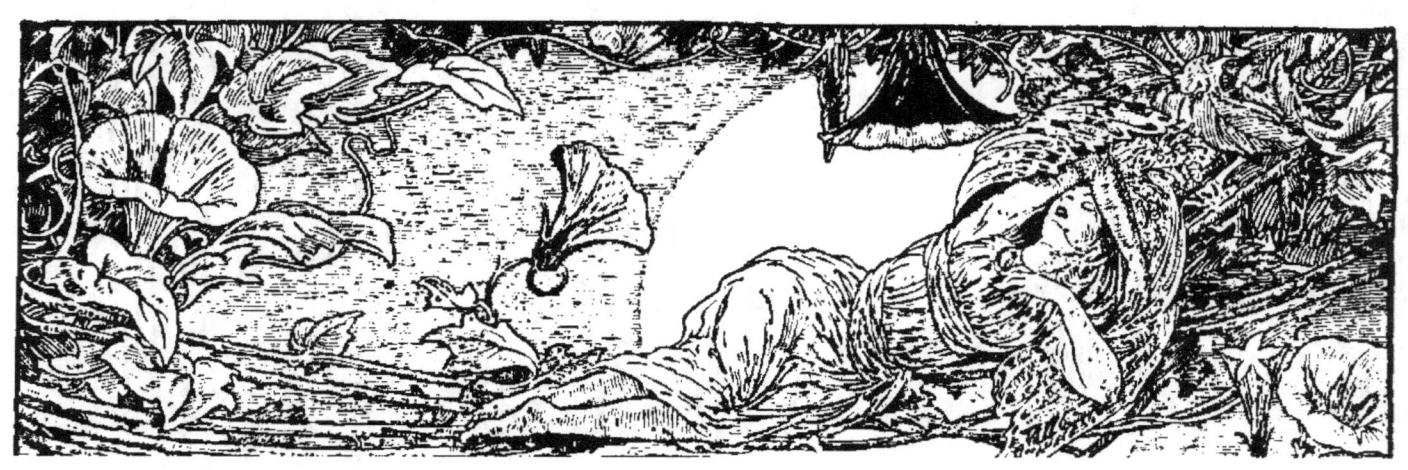

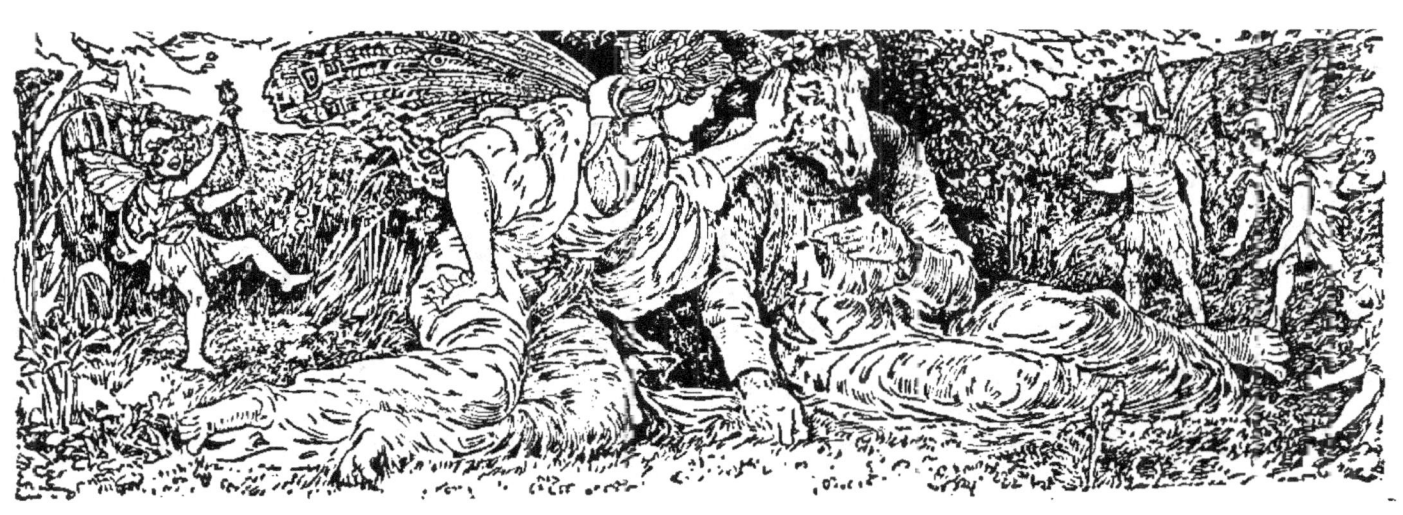

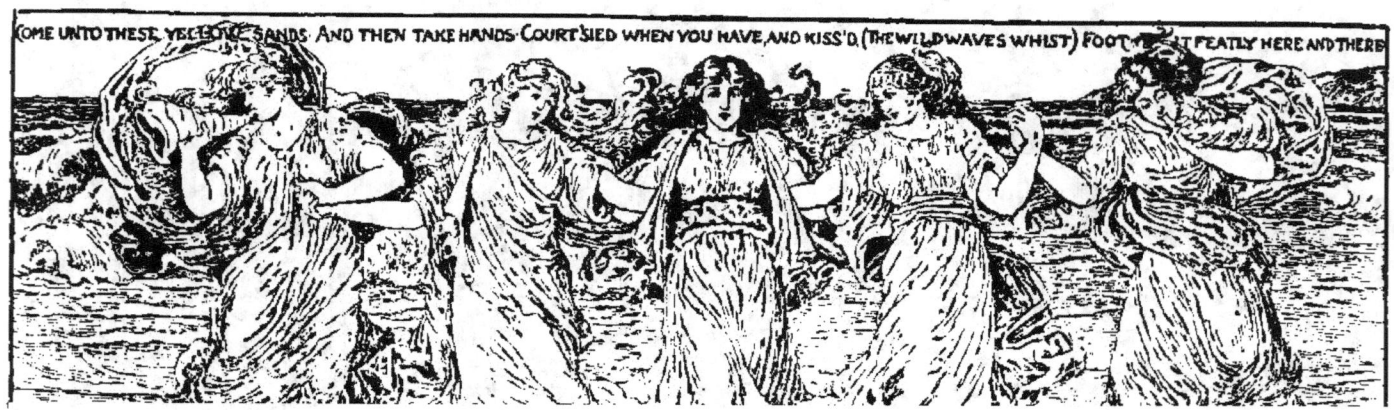

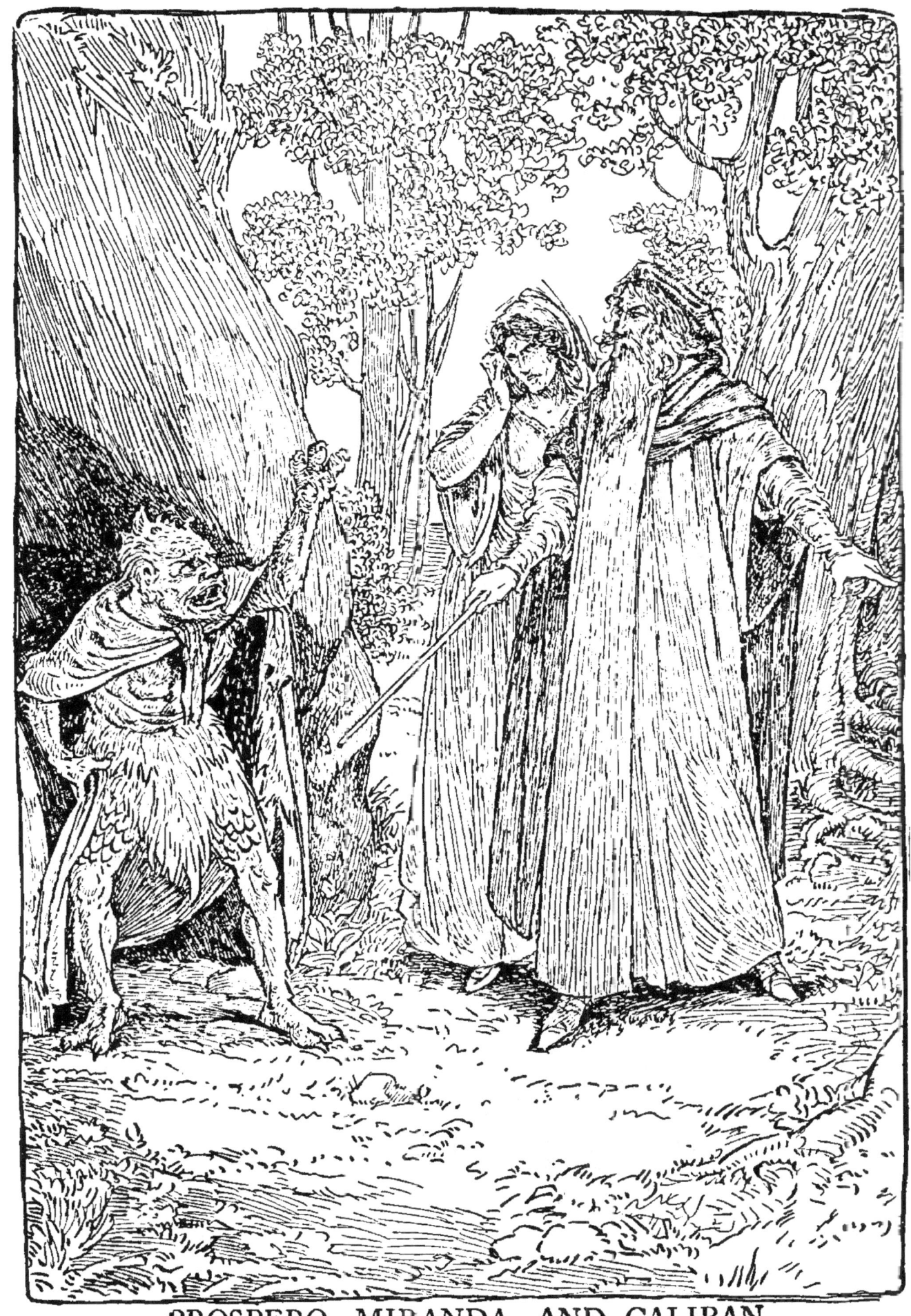
PROSPERO, MIRANDA, AND CALIBAN

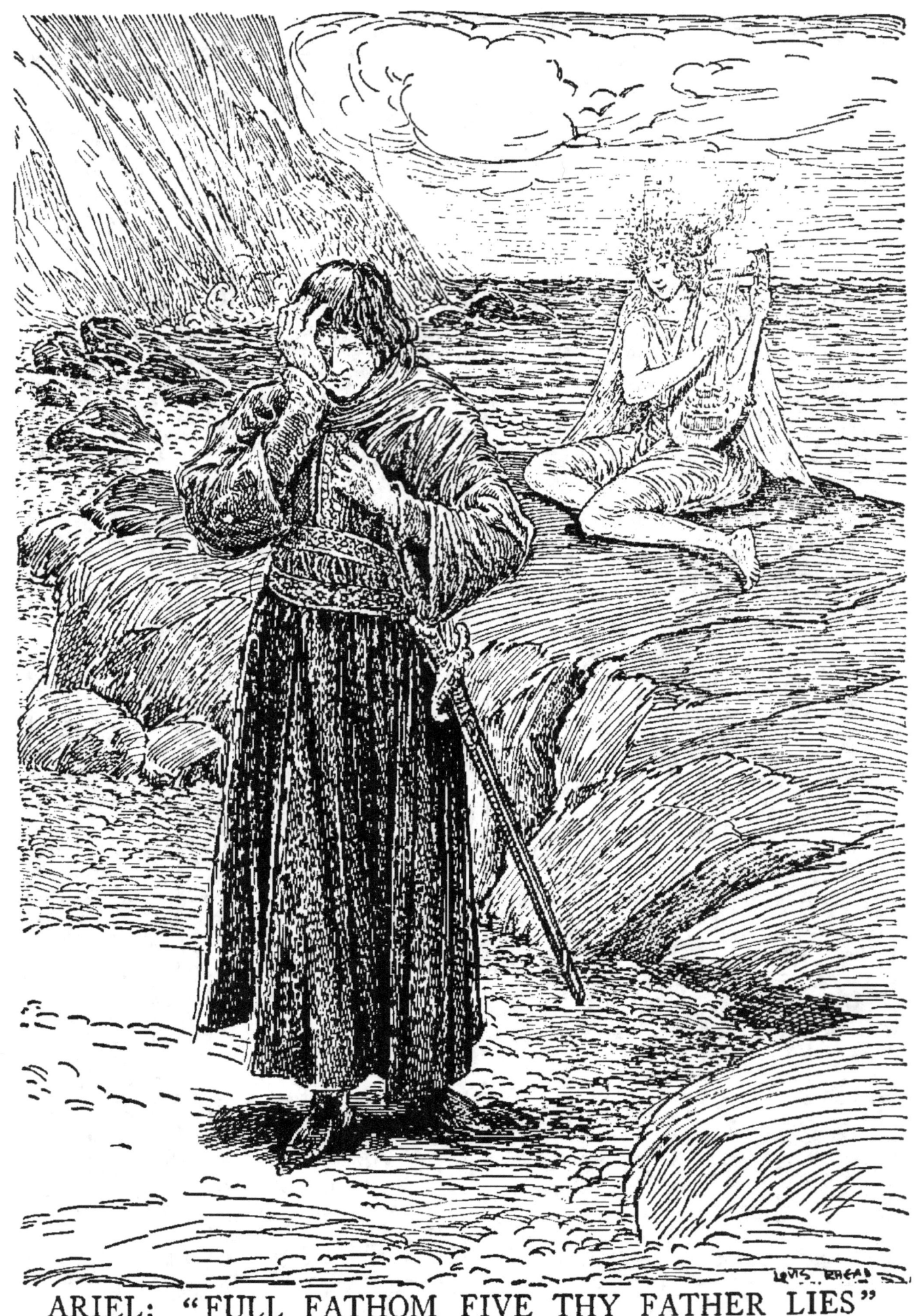

ARIEL: "FULL FATHOM FIVE THY FATHER LIES"

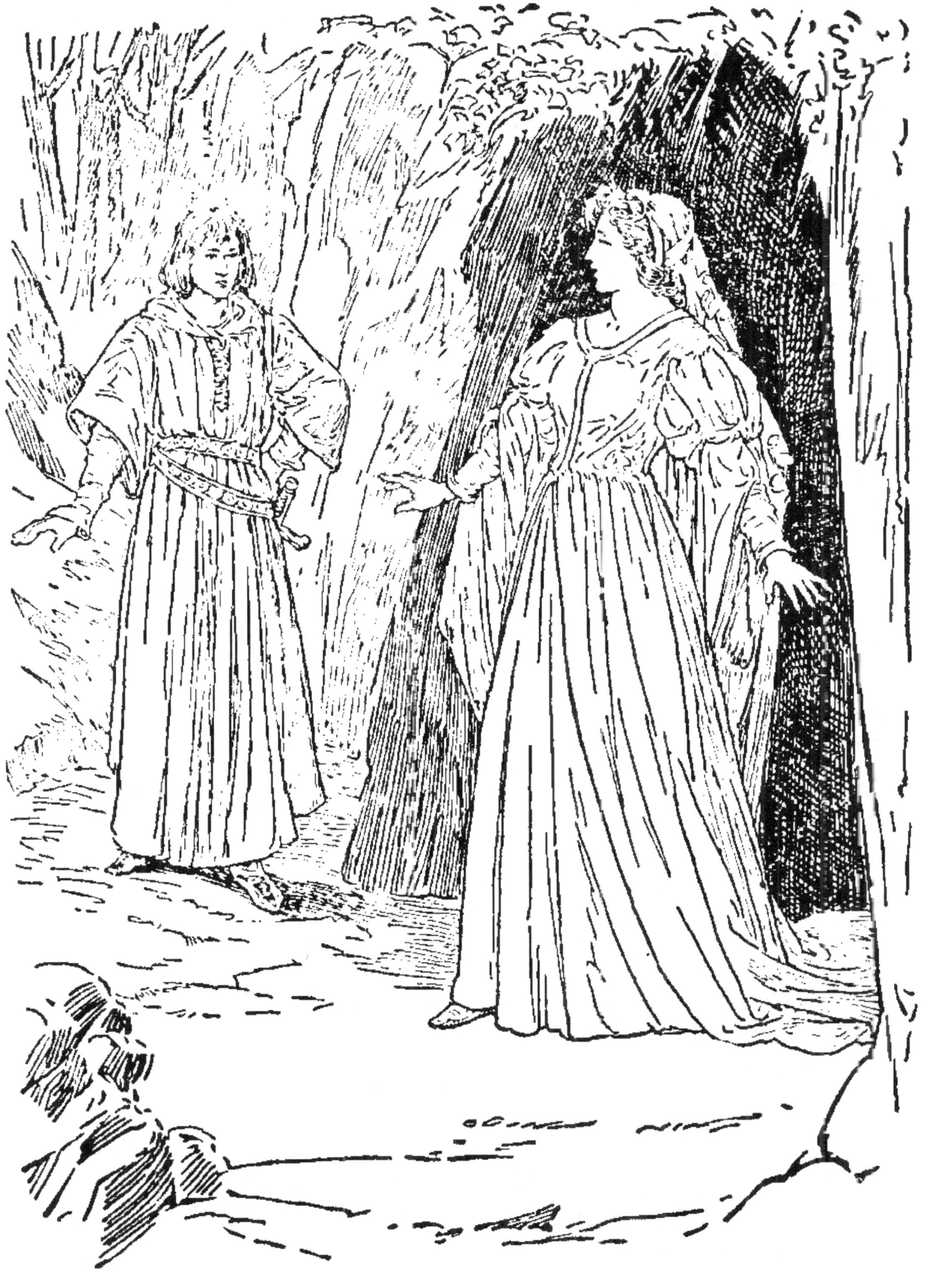

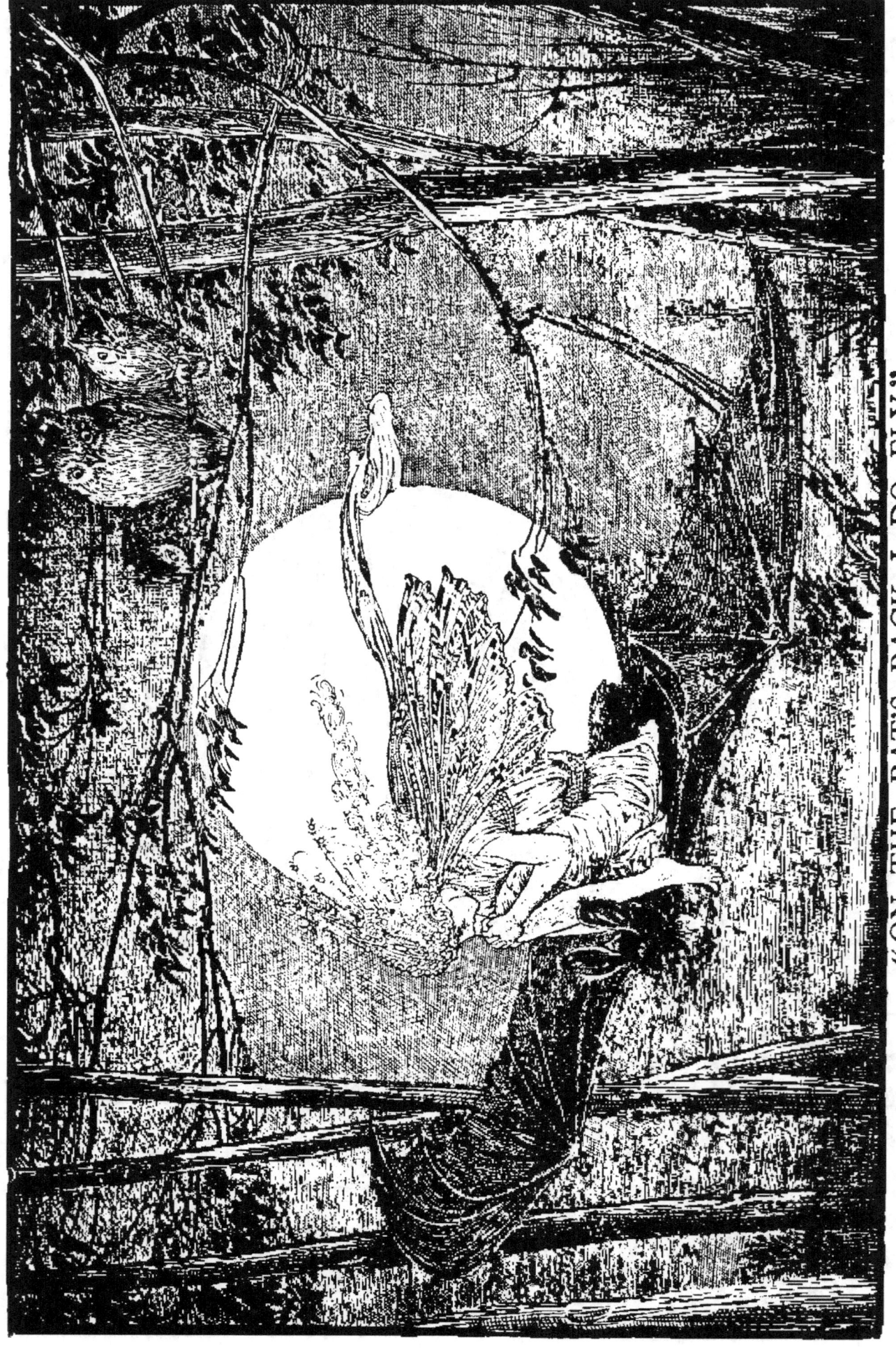

"ON THE BAT'S BACK I DO FLY"

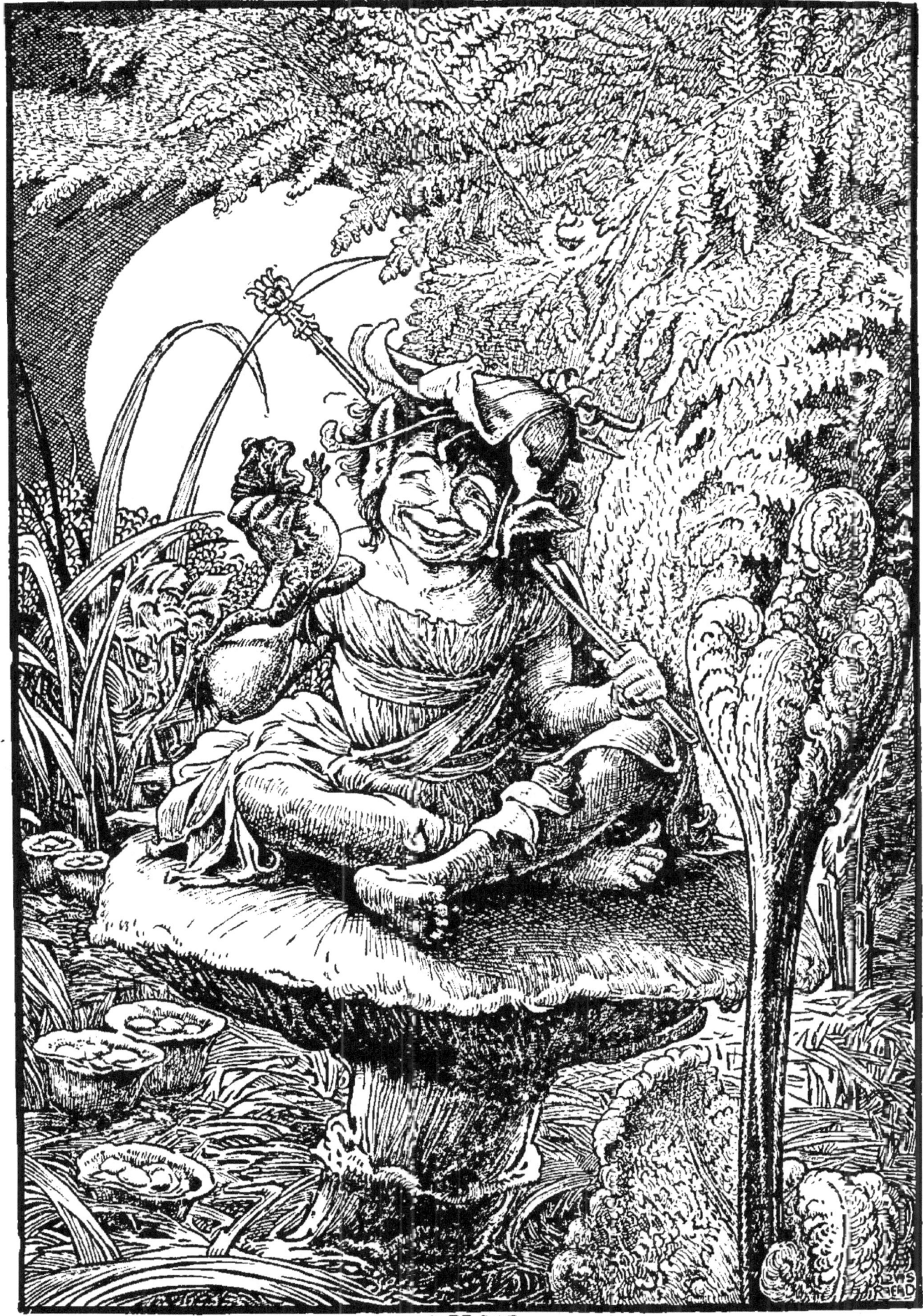

PUCK

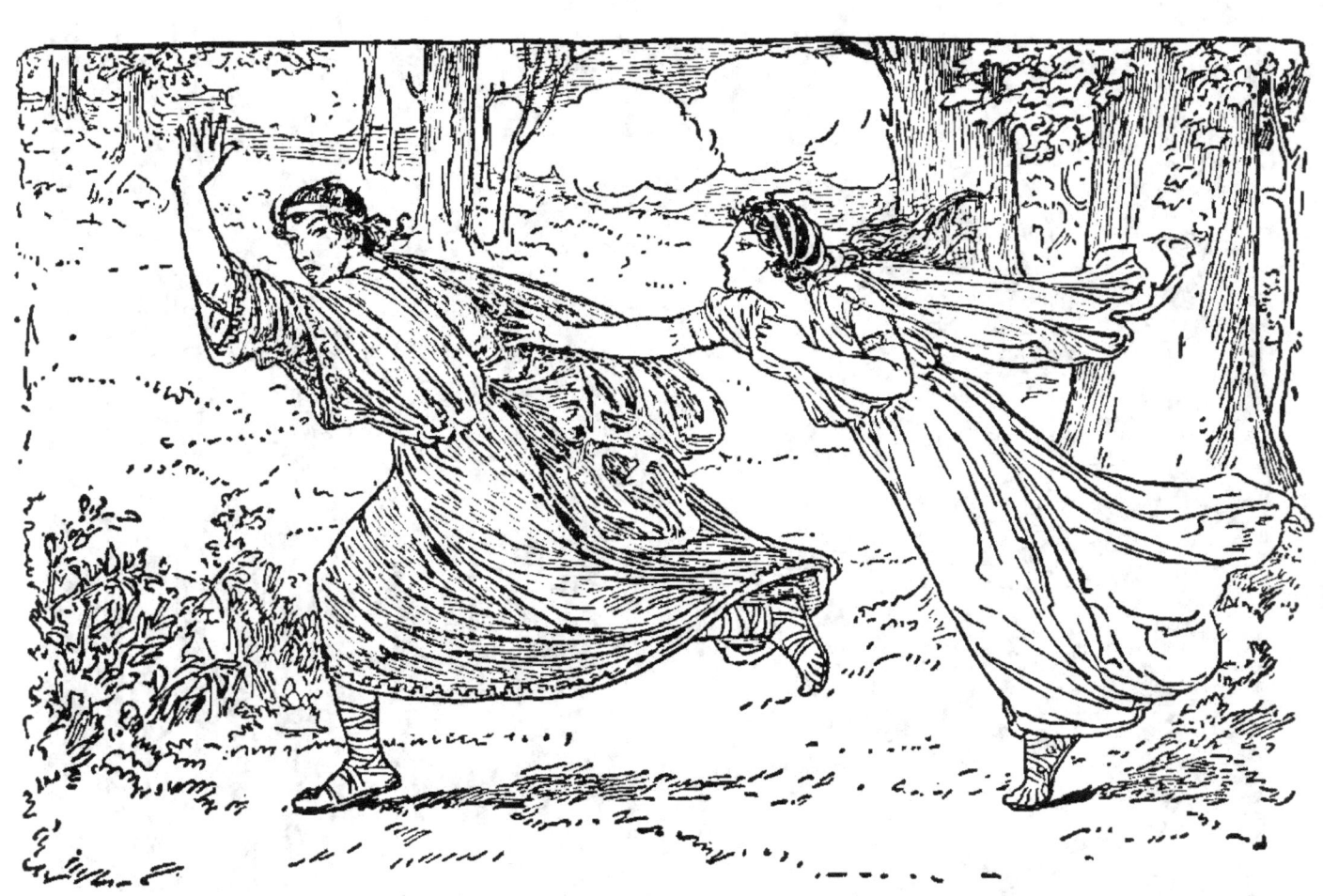

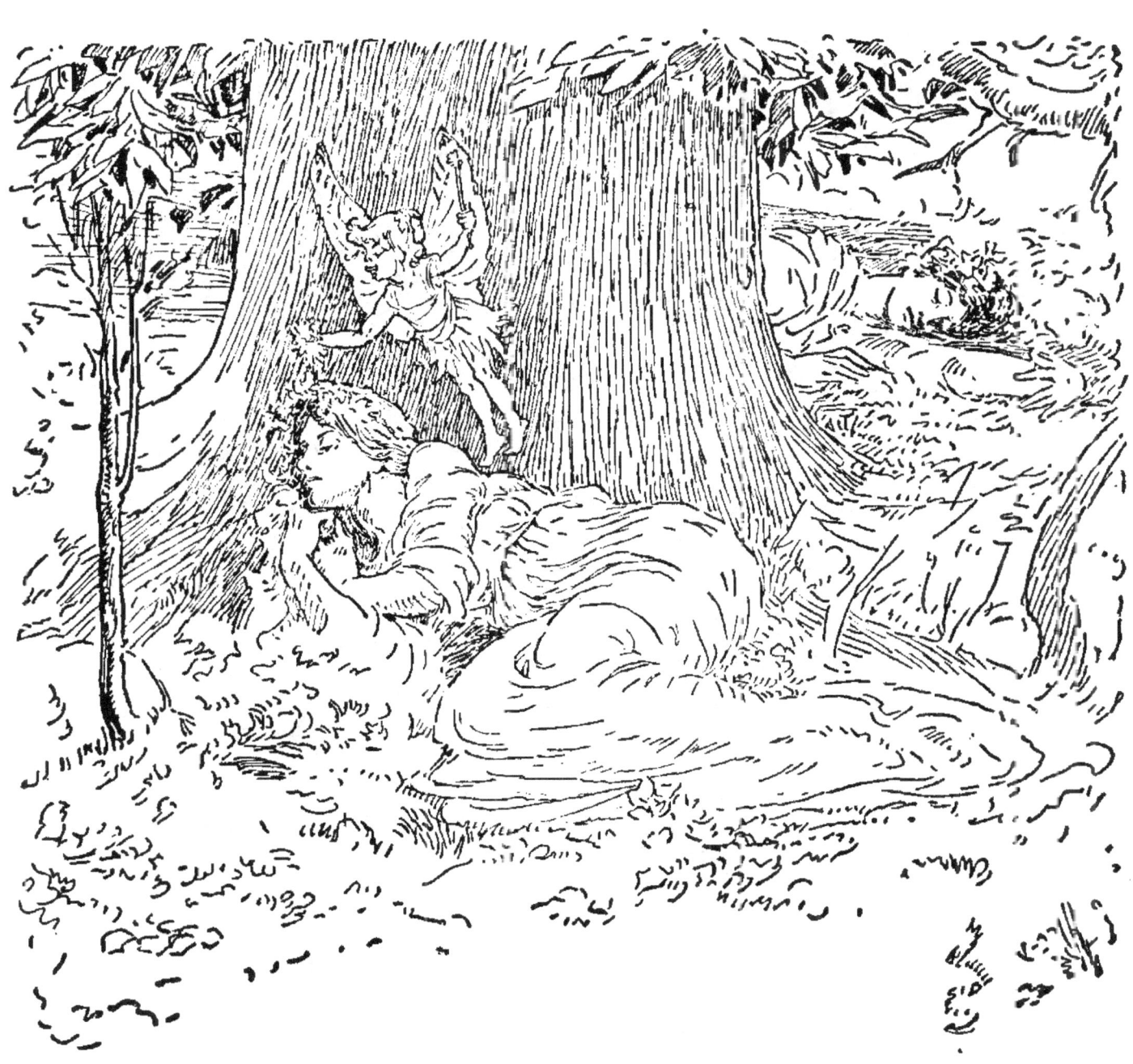

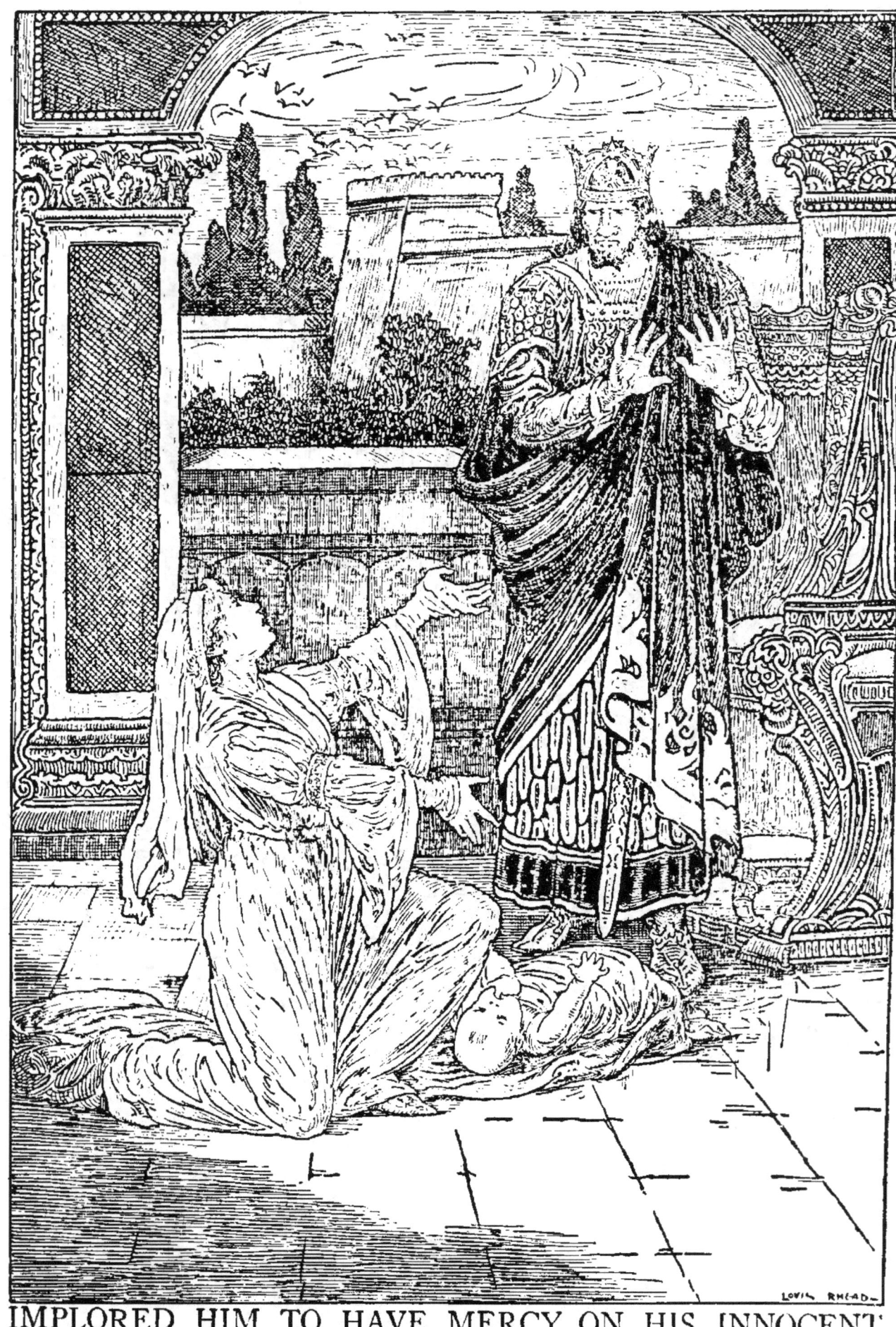

IMPLORED HIM TO HAVE MERCY ON HIS INNOCENT WIFE AND CHILD

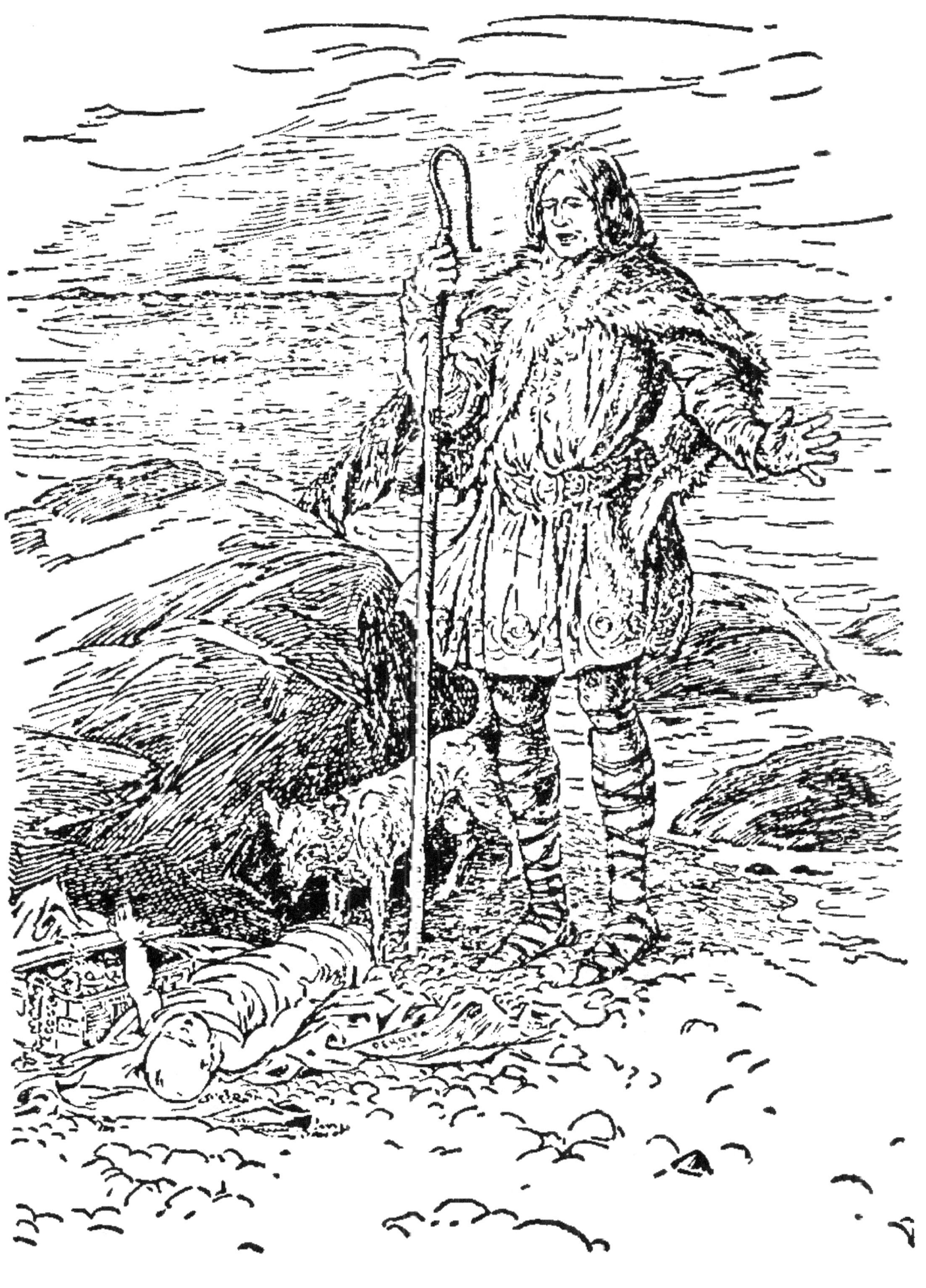

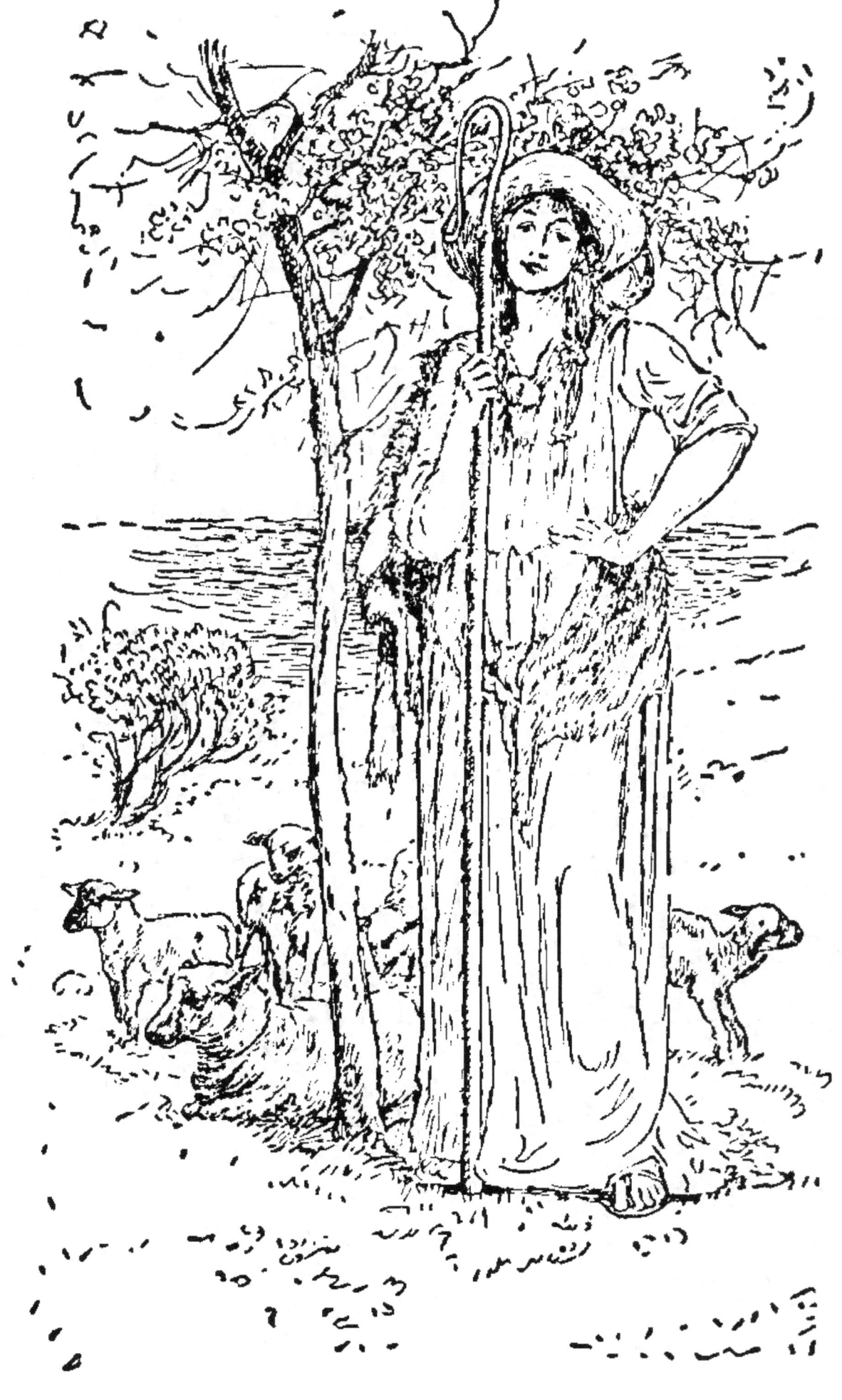

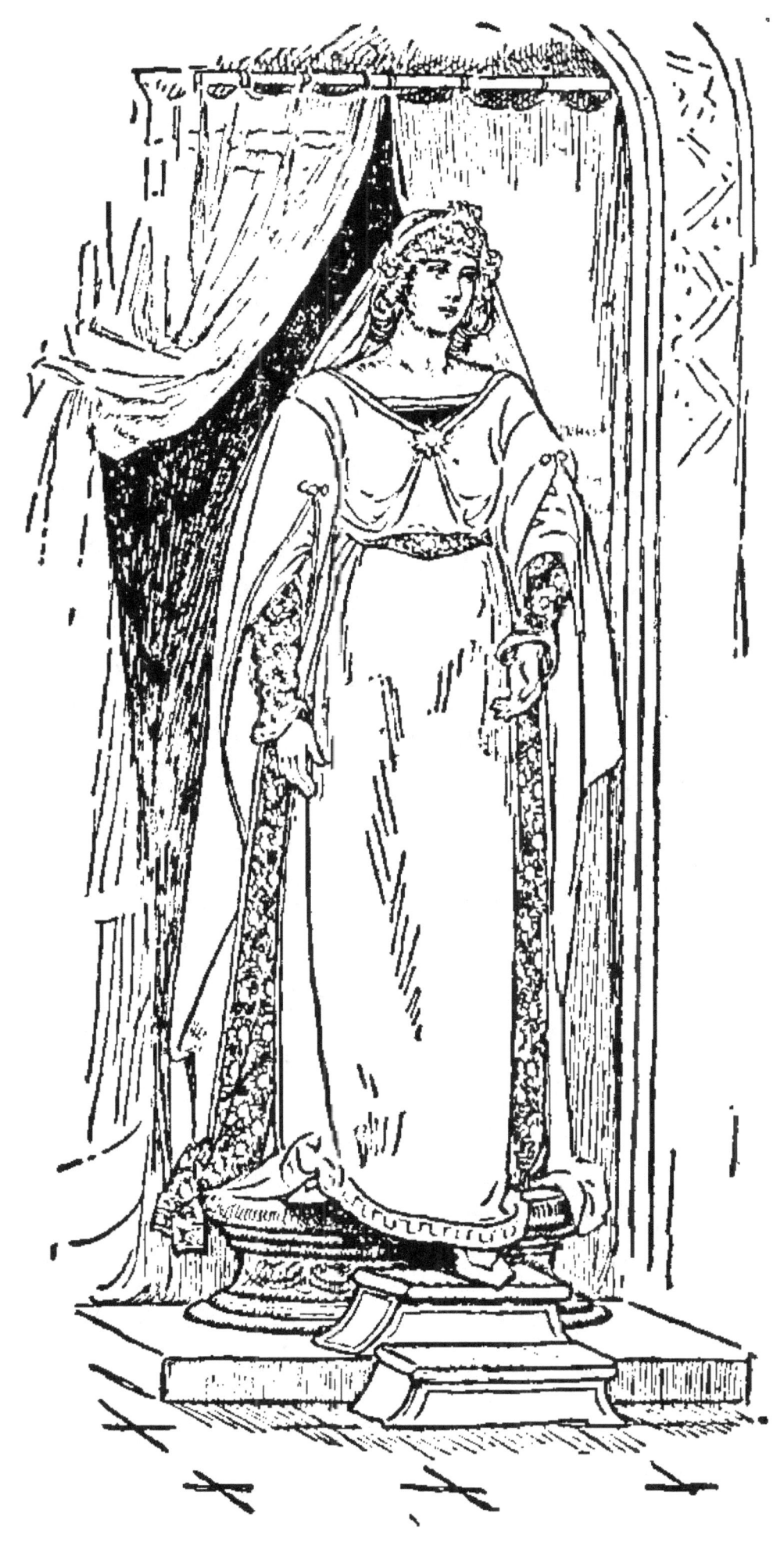

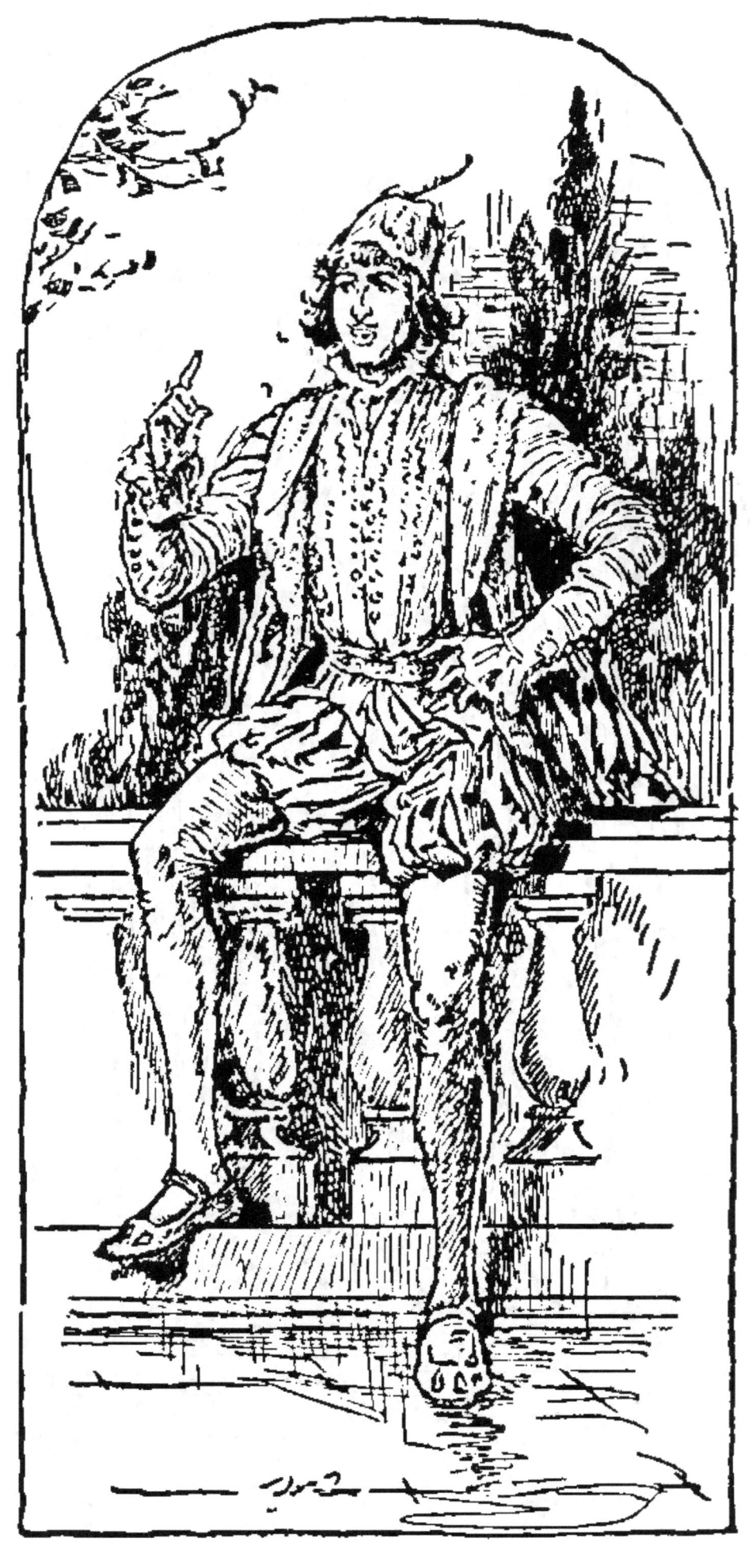

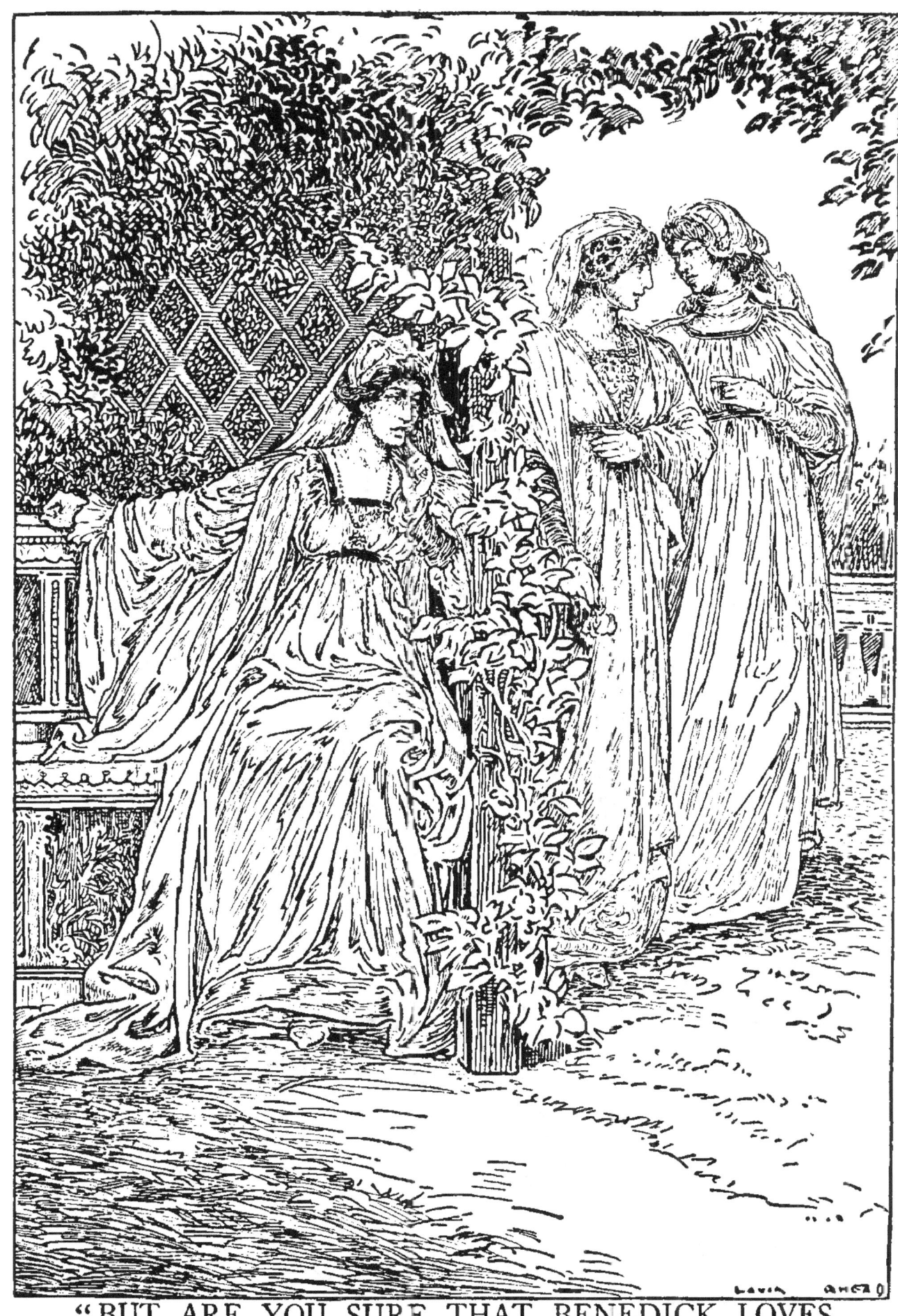

"BUT ARE YOU SURE THAT BENEDICK LOVES BEATRICE SO ENTIRELY?"

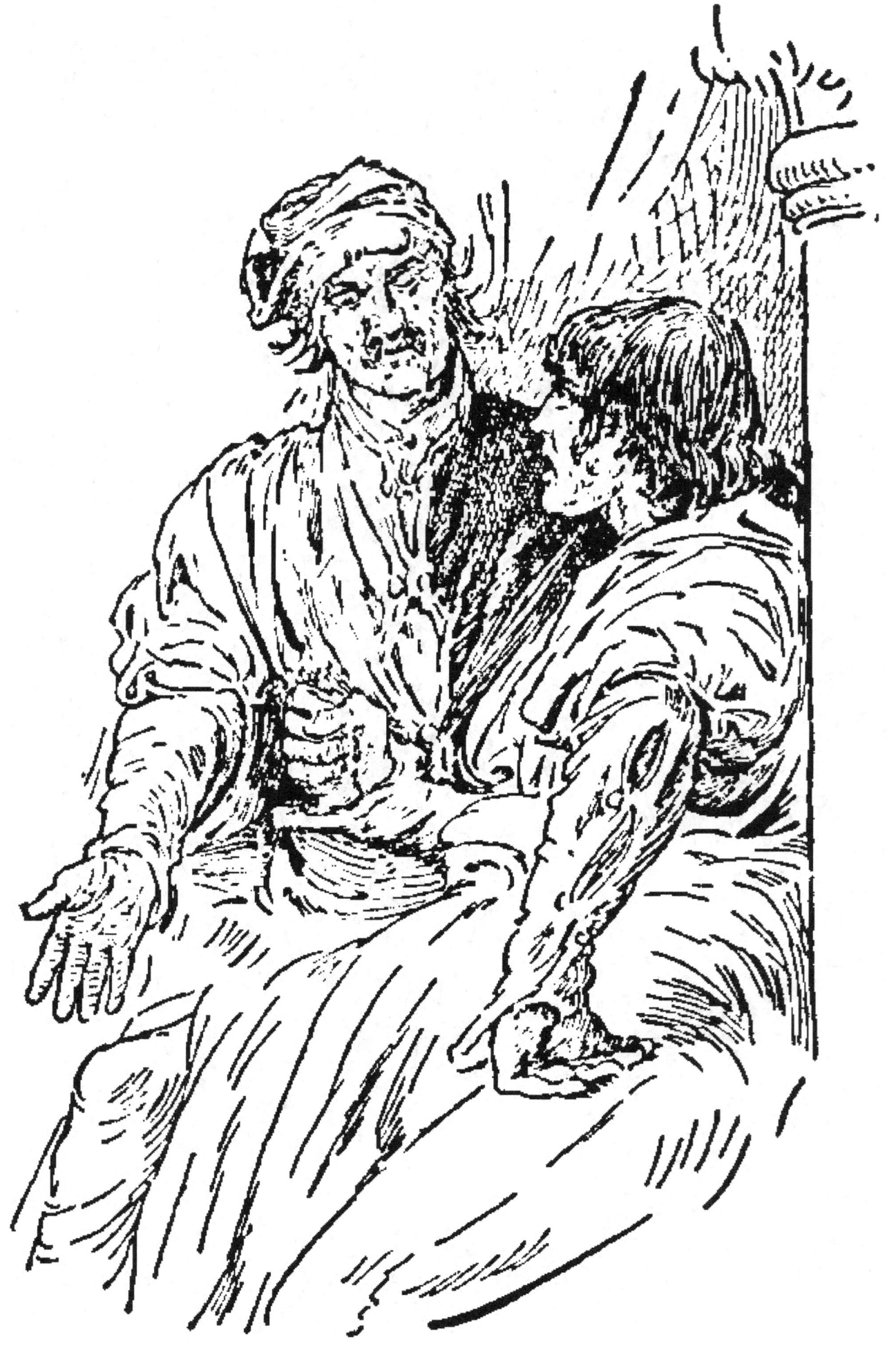

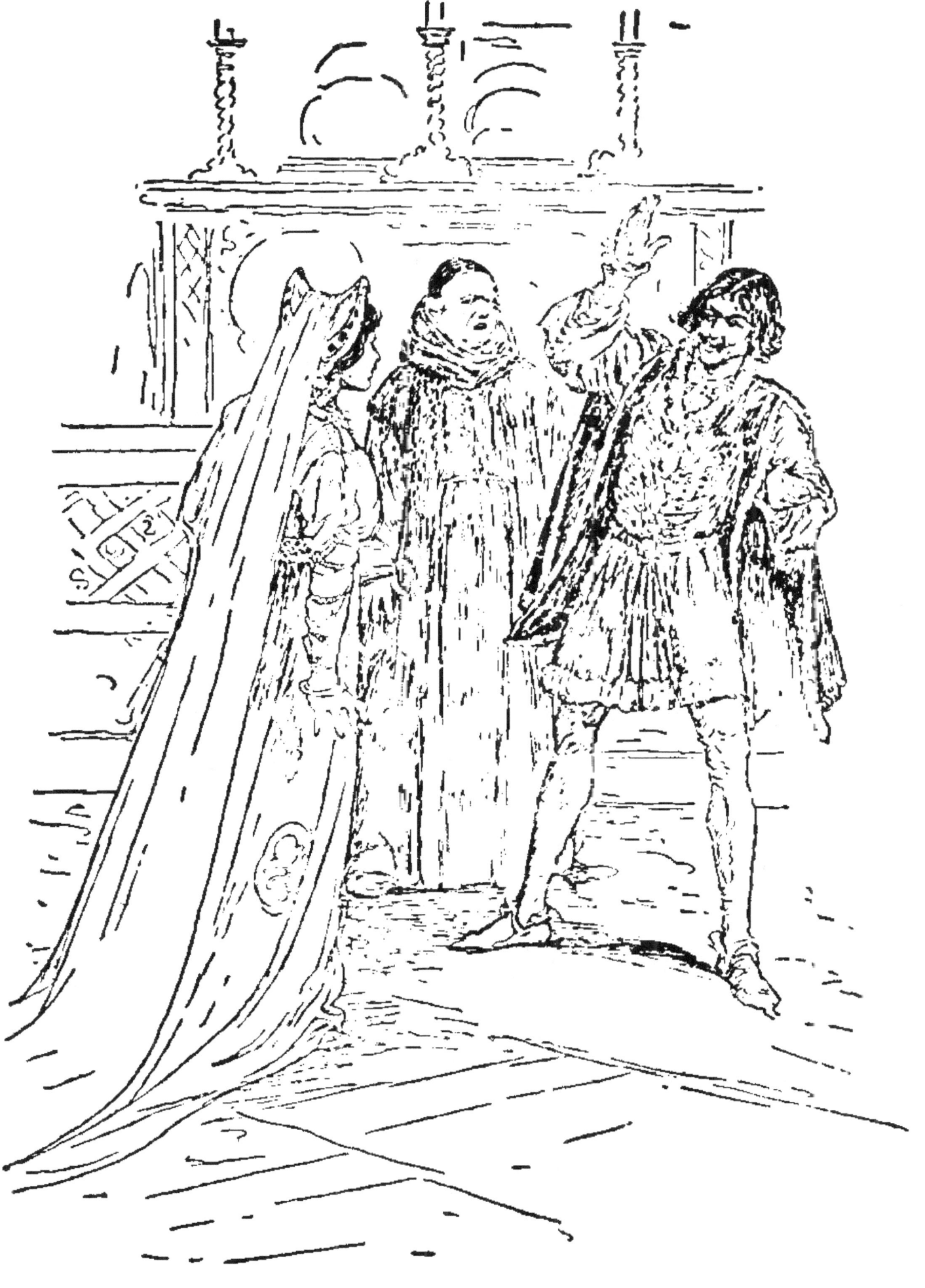

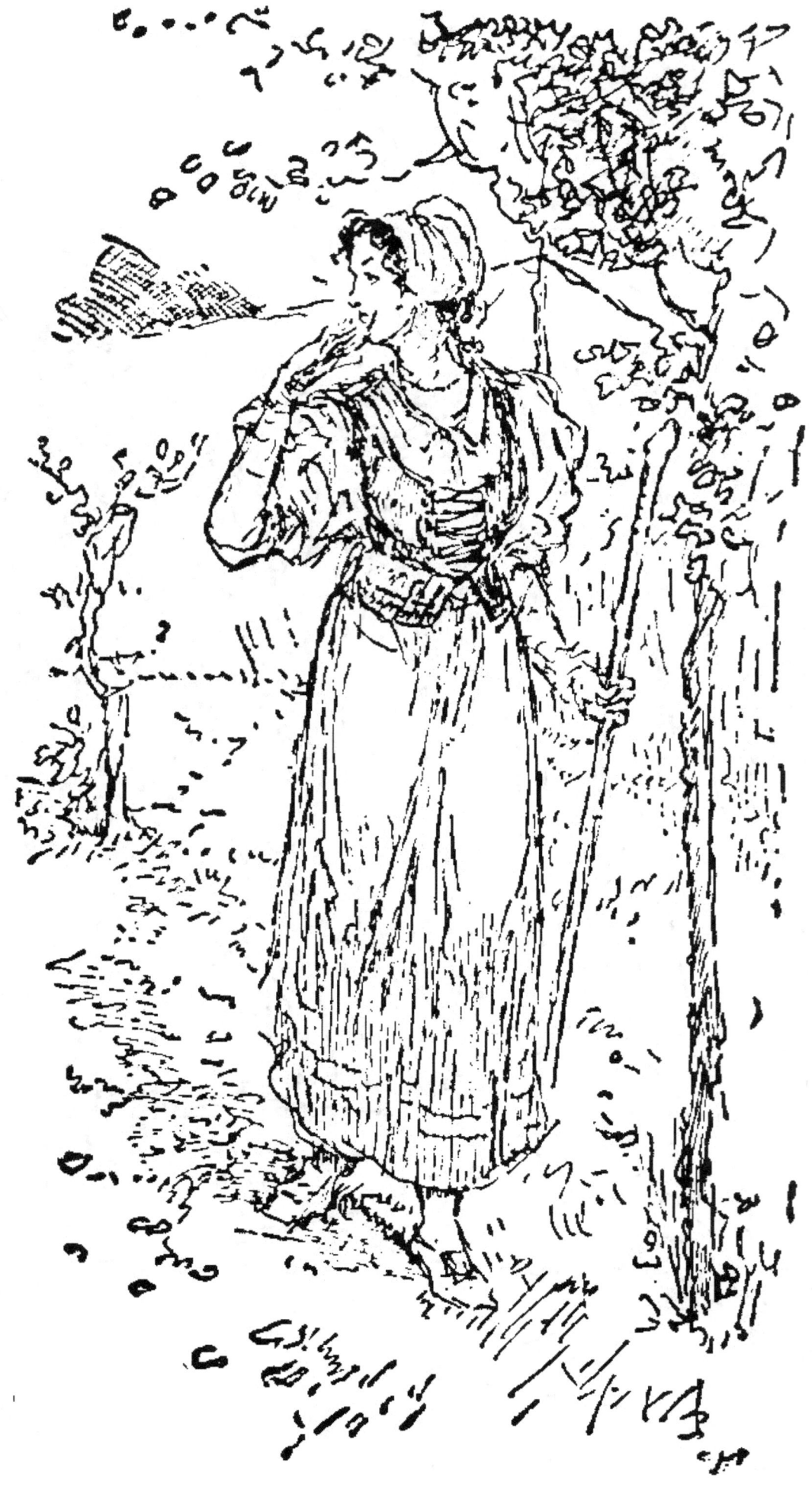

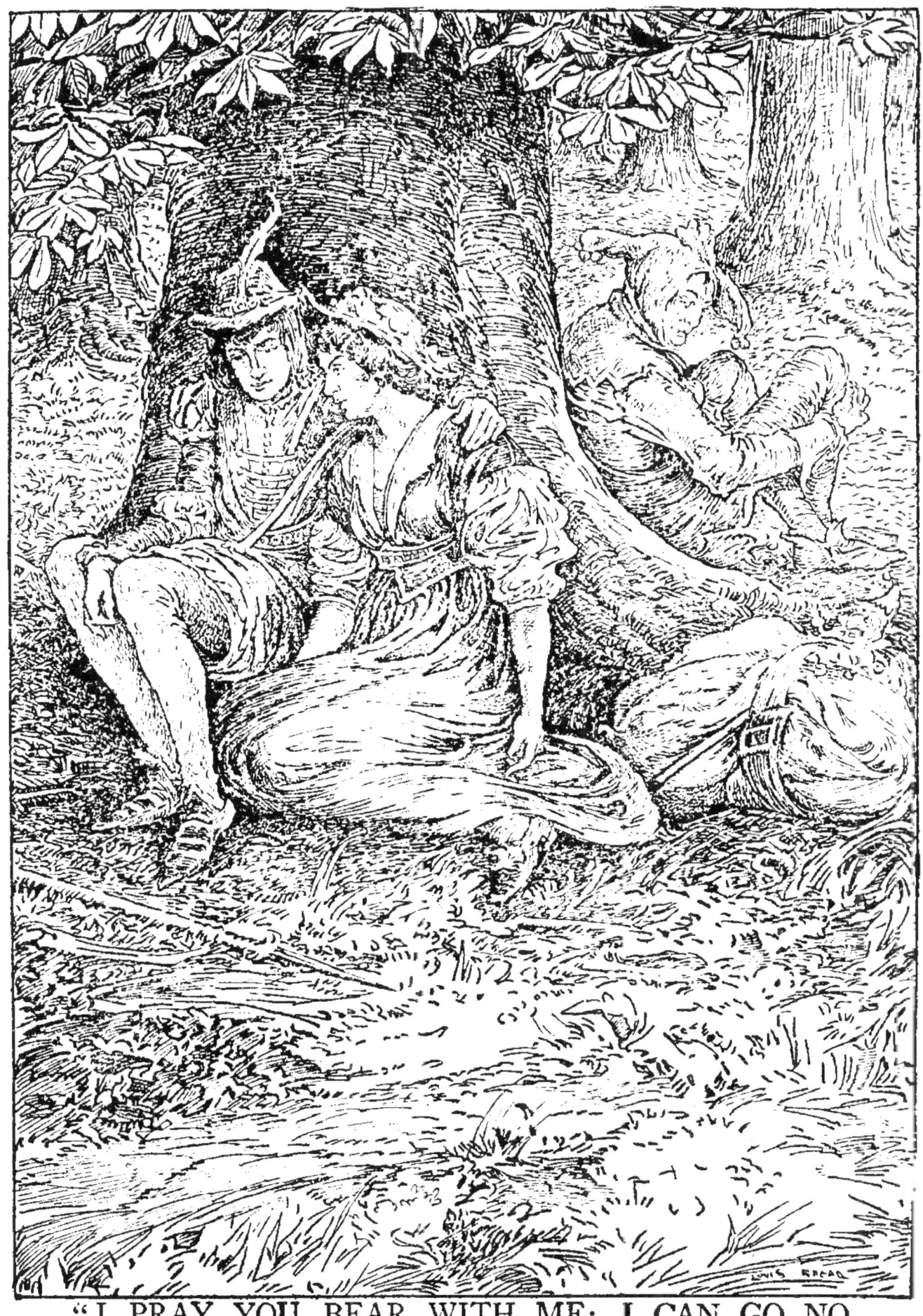

"I PRAY YOU, BEAR WITH ME; I CAN GO NO FURTHER"

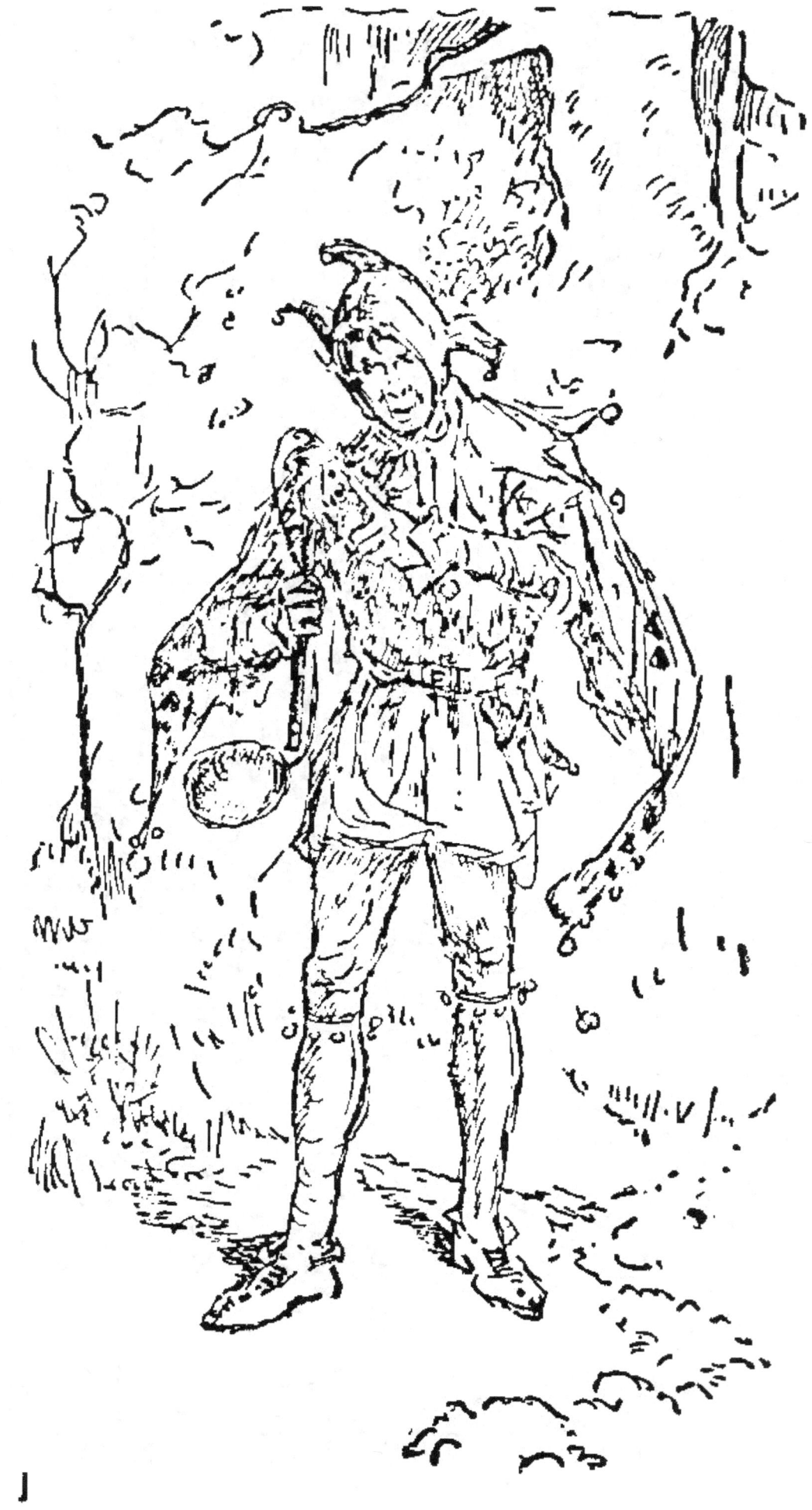

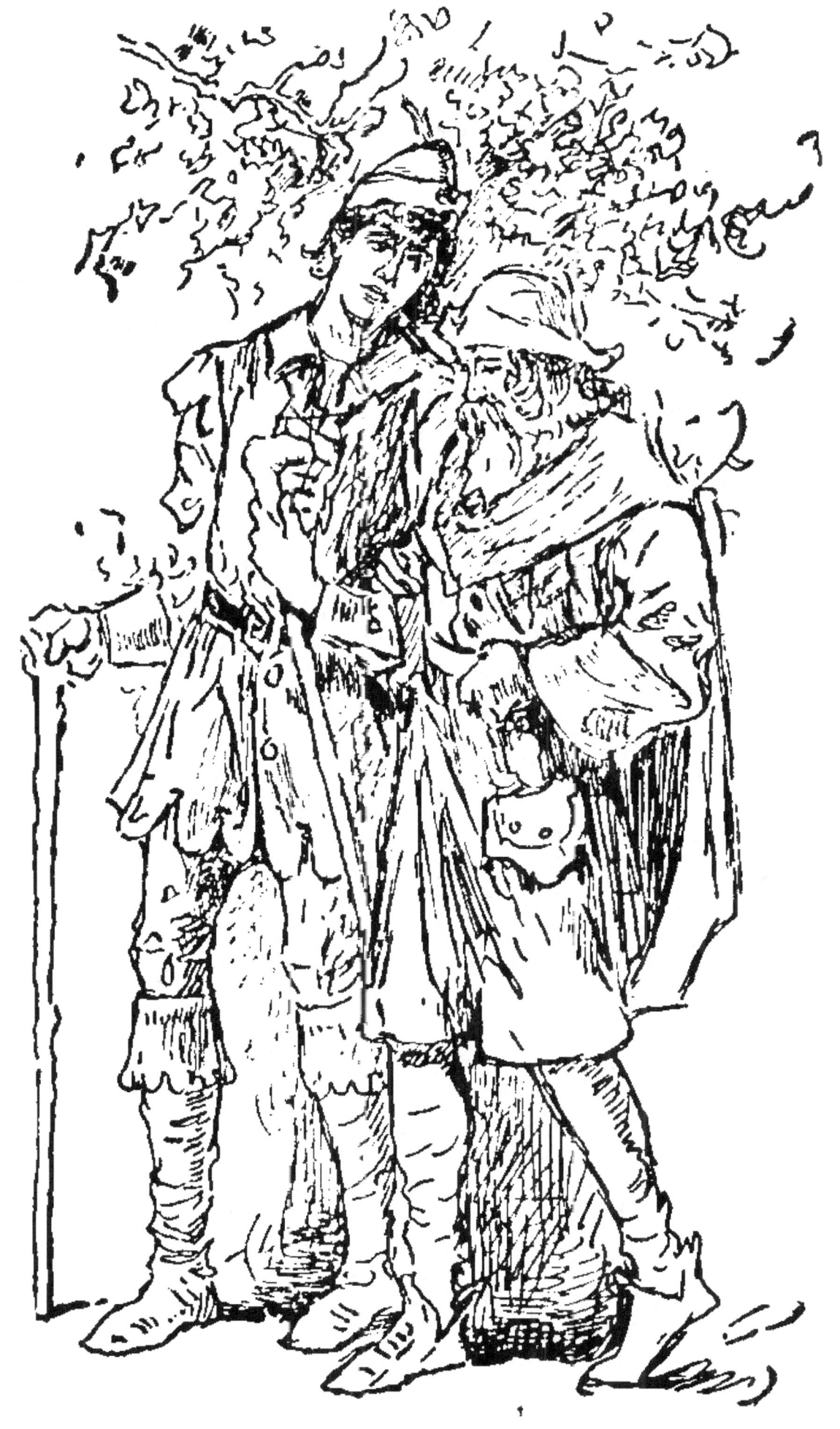

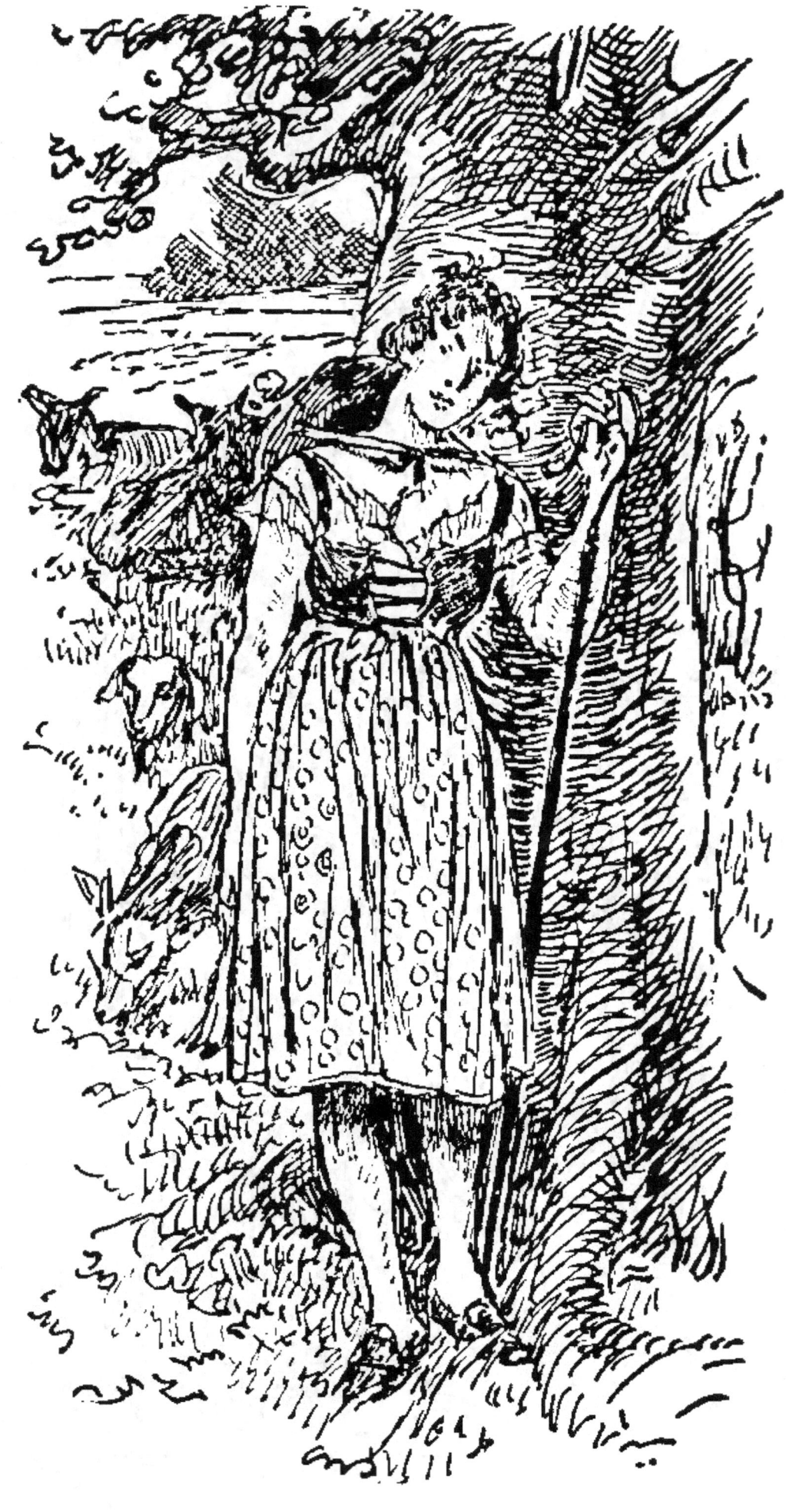

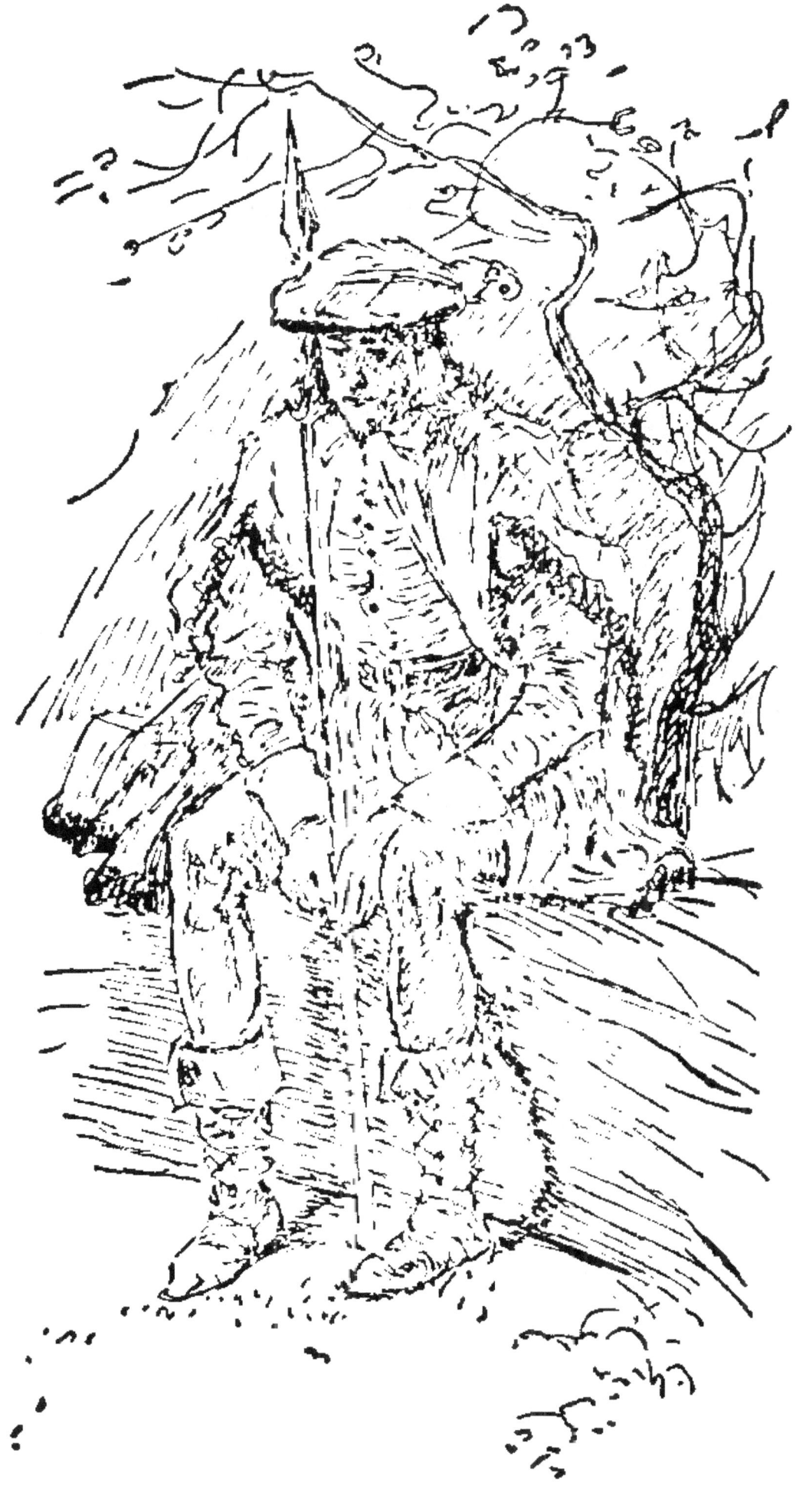

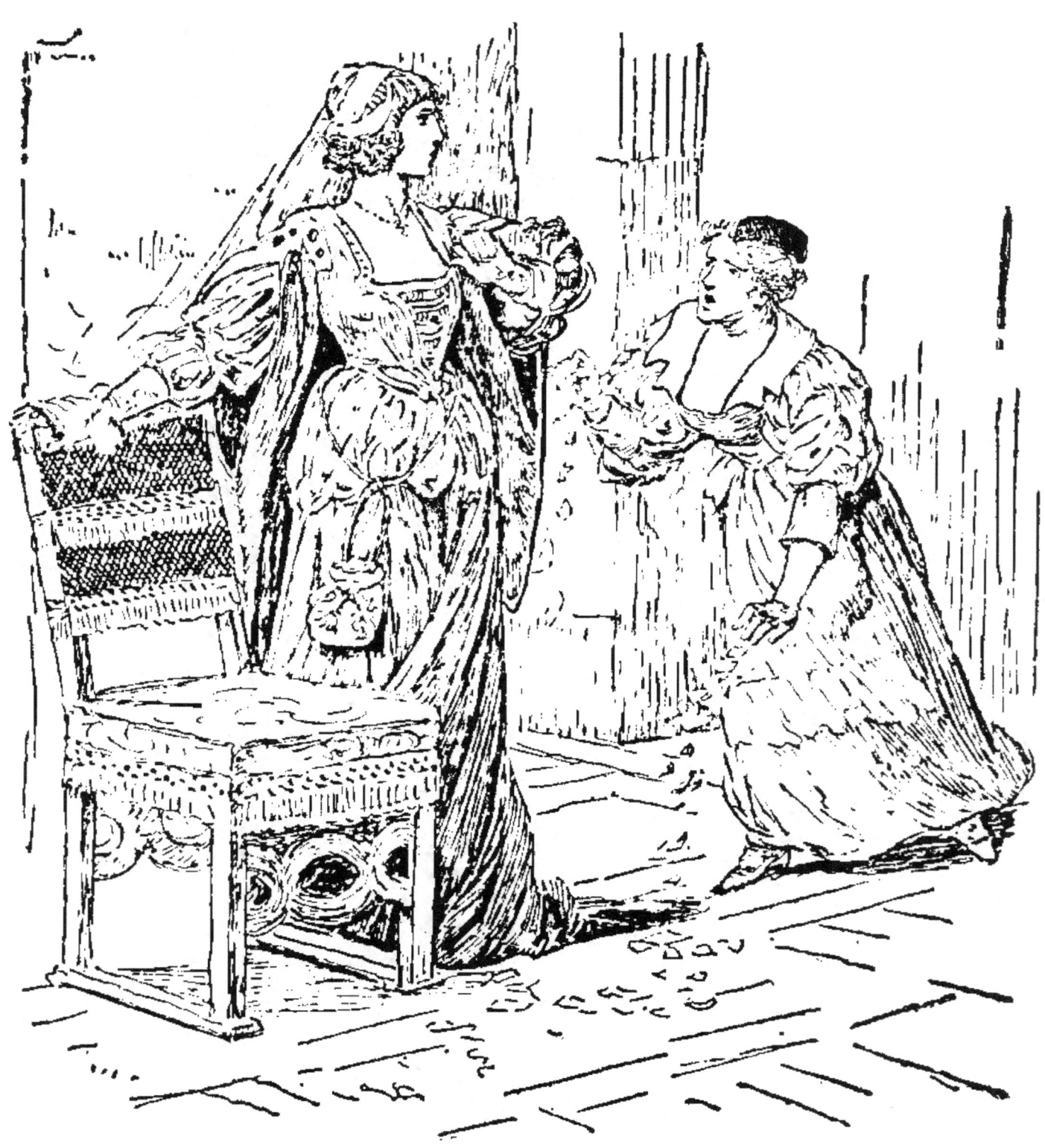

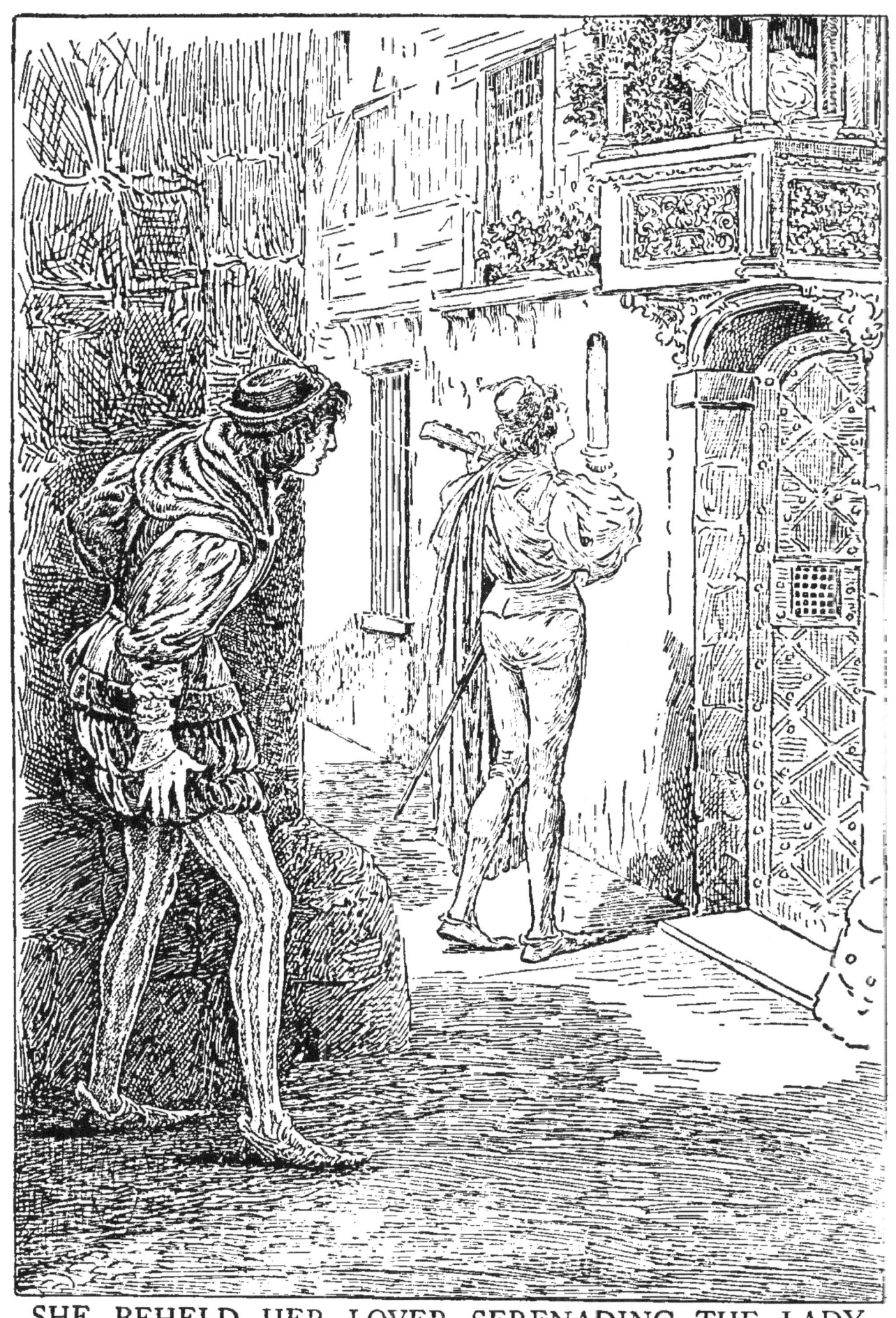

SHE BEHELD HER LOVER SERENADING THE LADY
SILVIA WITH MUSIC

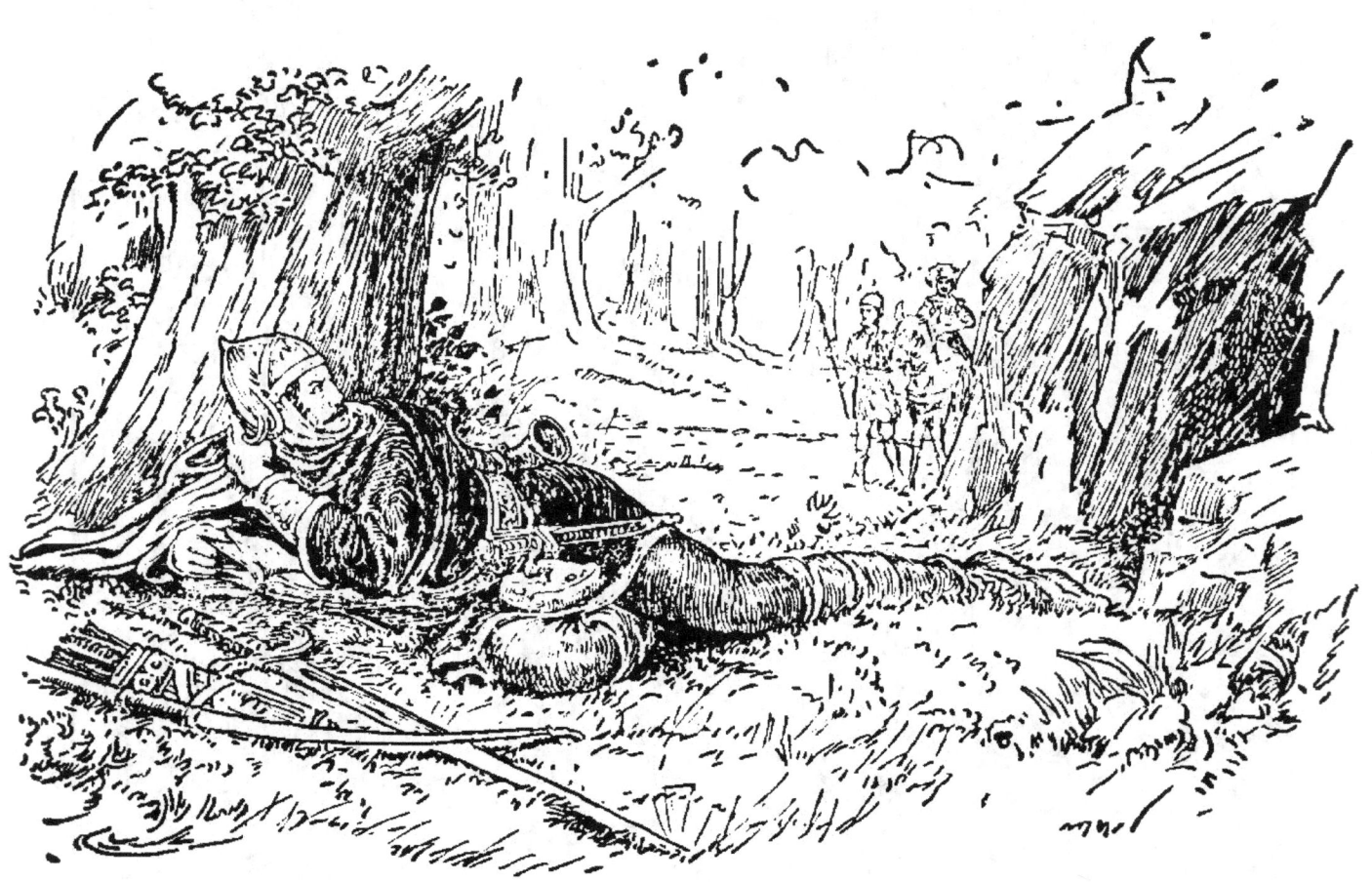

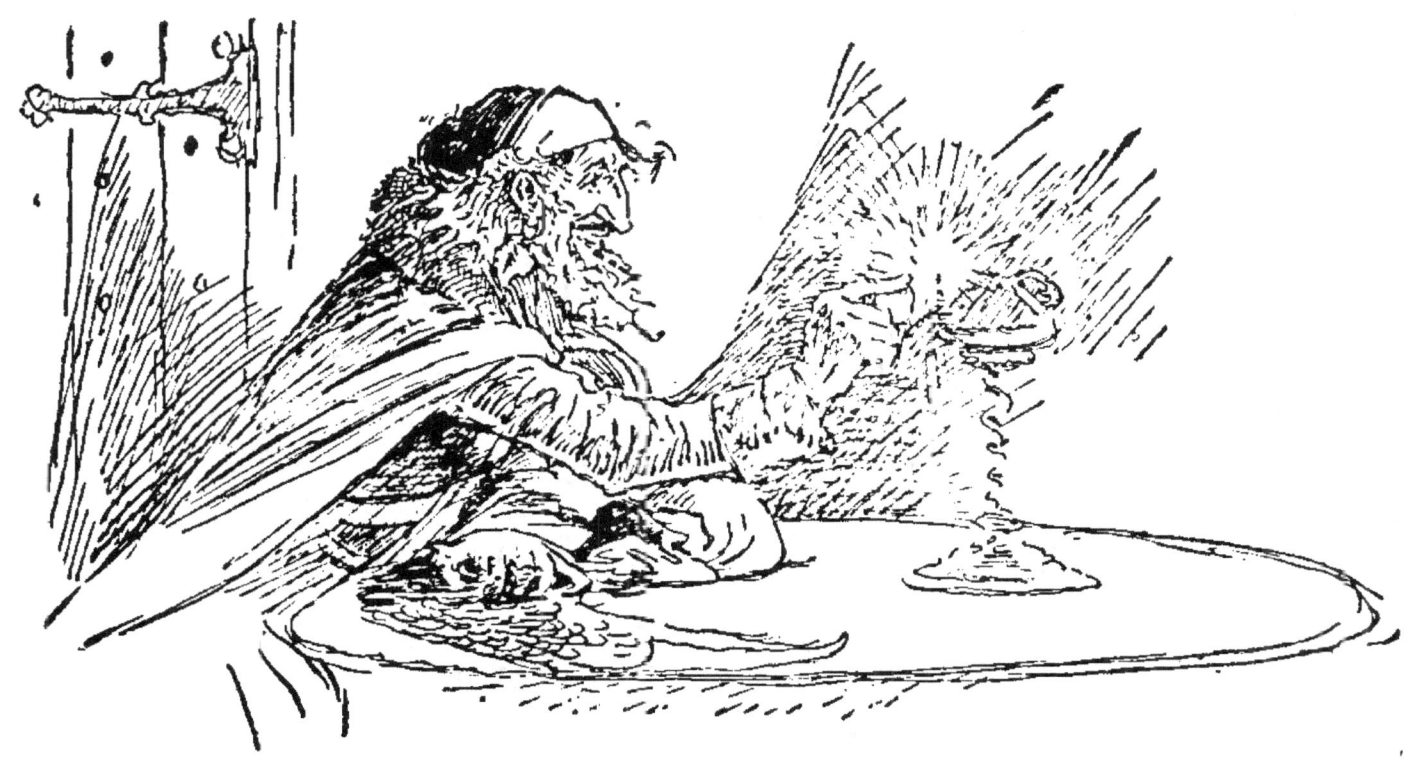

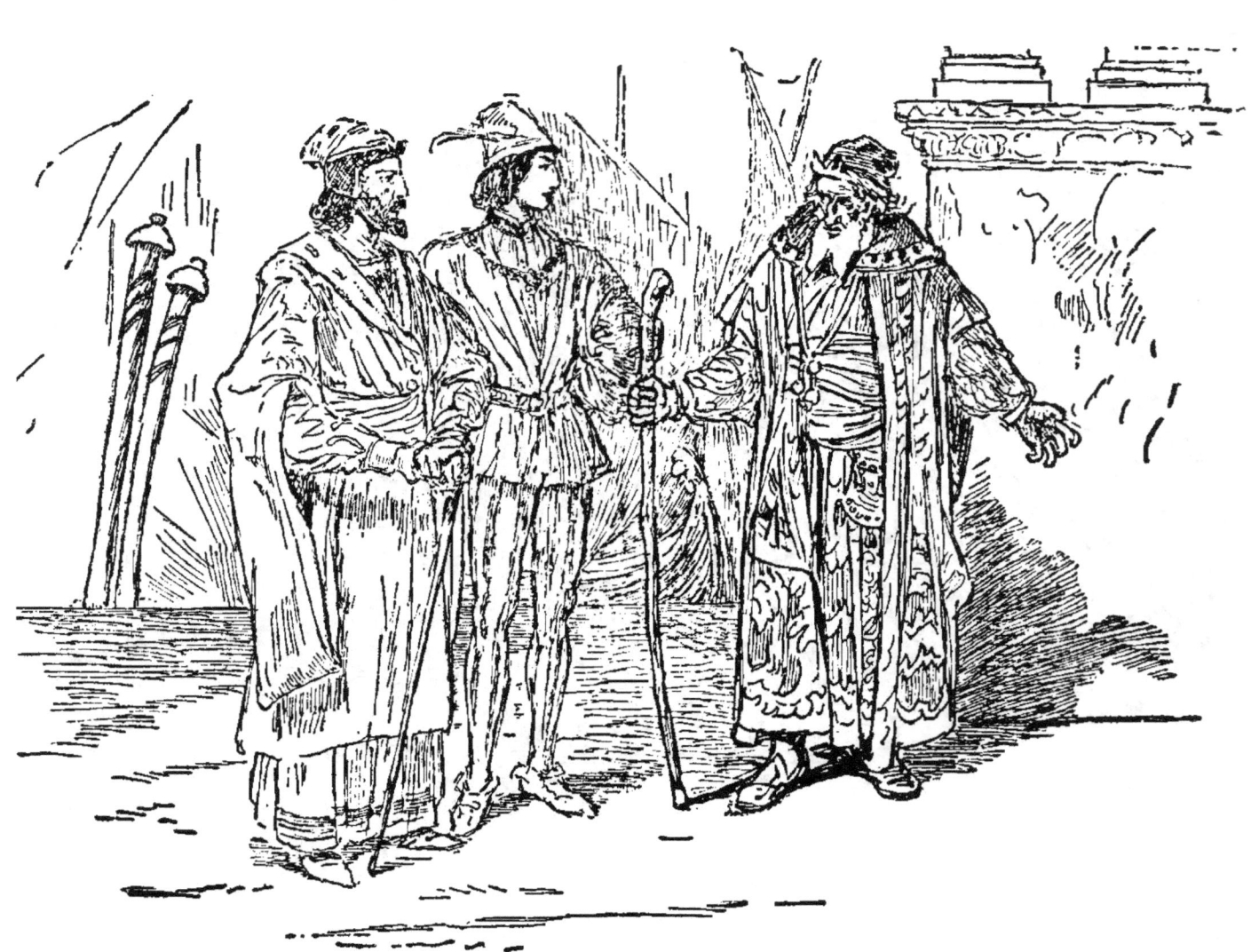

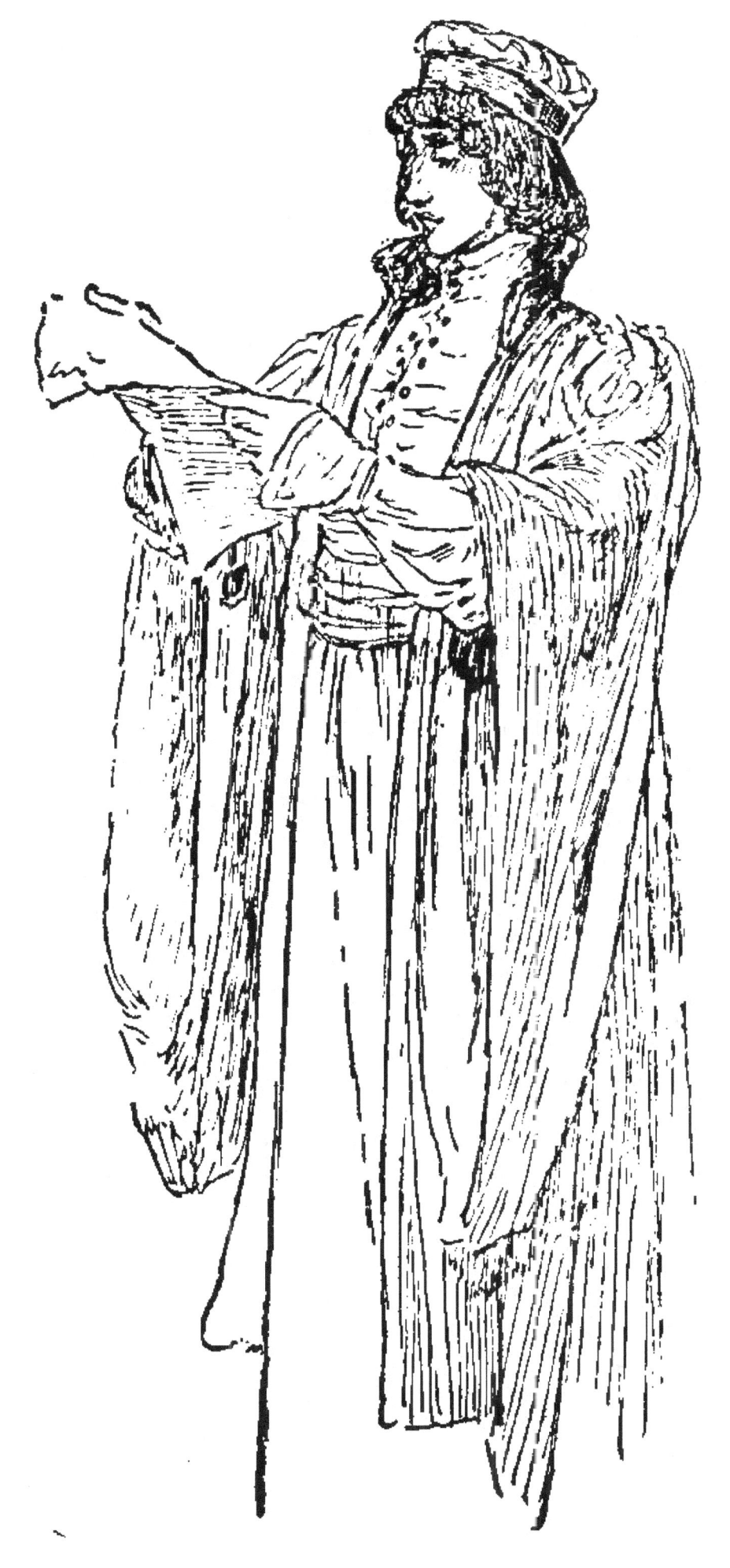

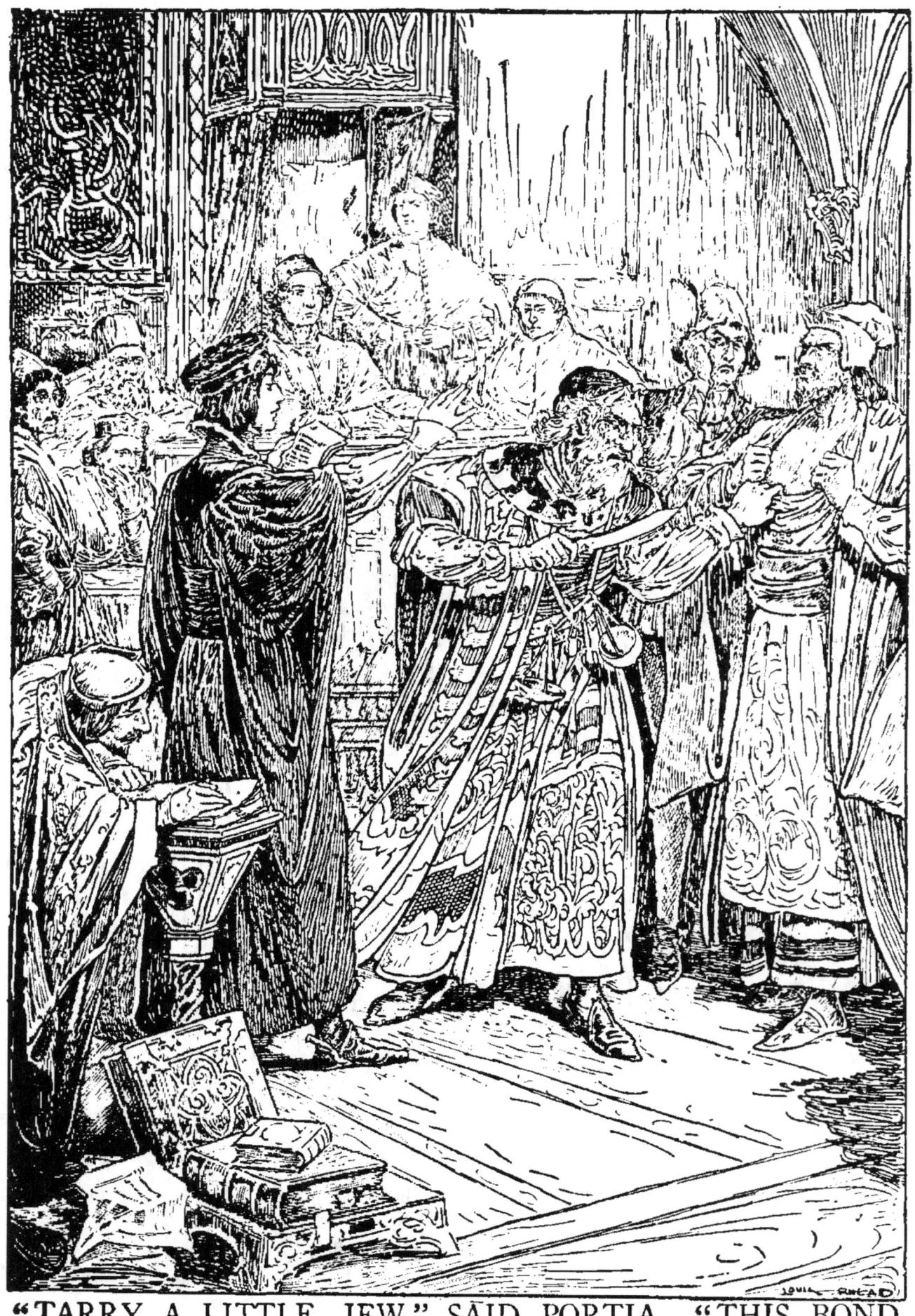

"TARRY A LITTLE, JEW," SAID PORTIA. "THIS BOND HERE GIVES YOU NO DROP OF BLOOD"

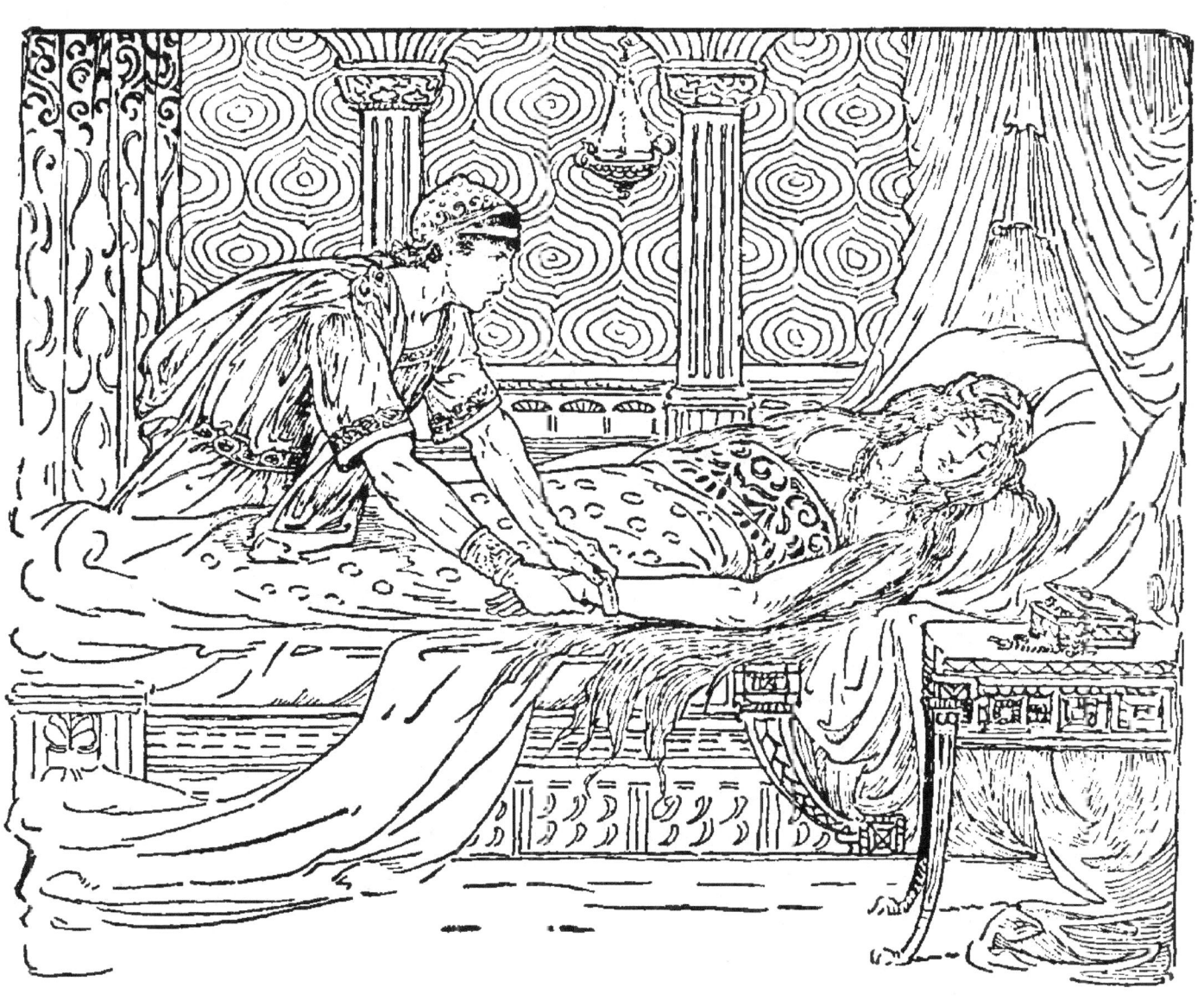

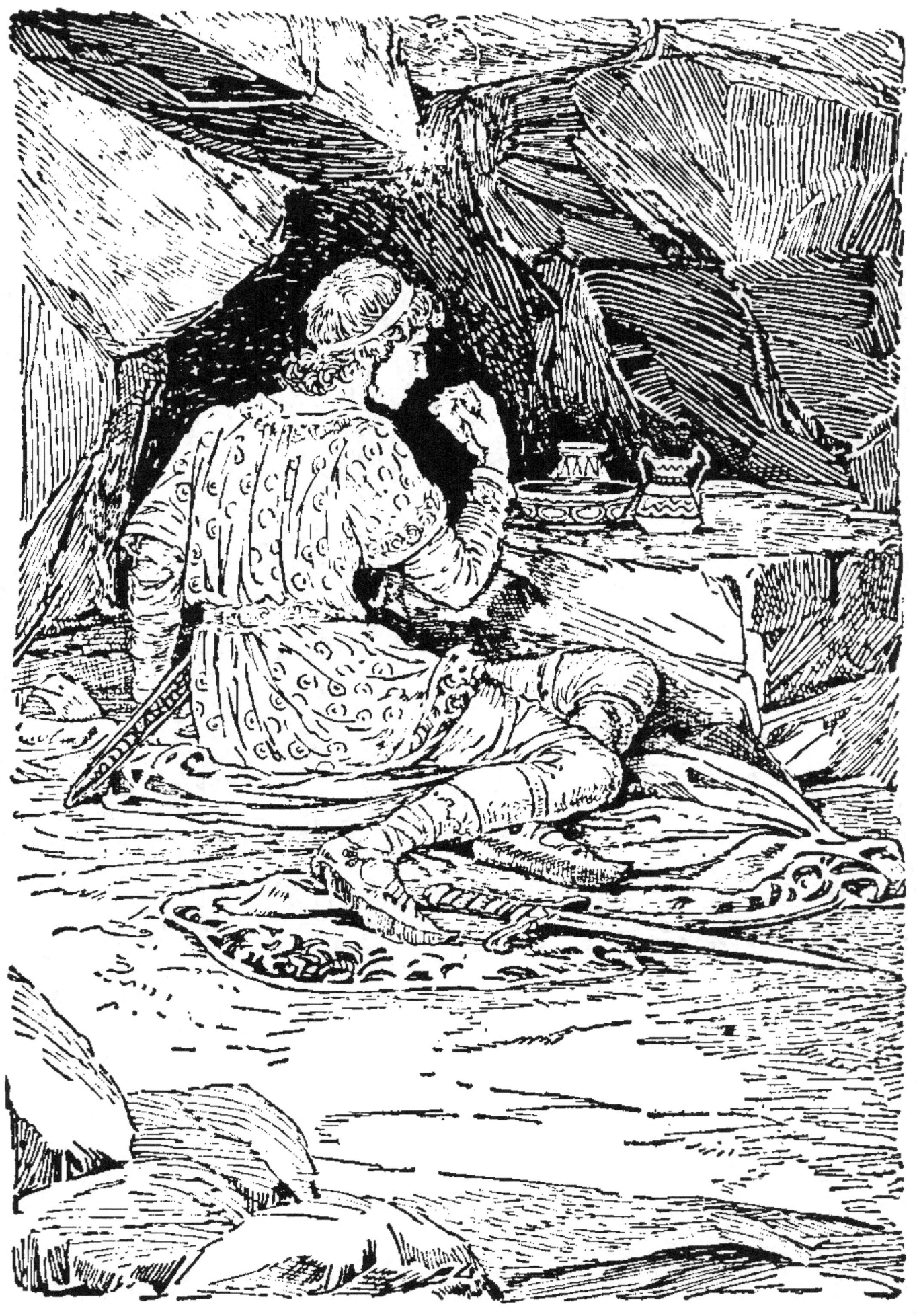

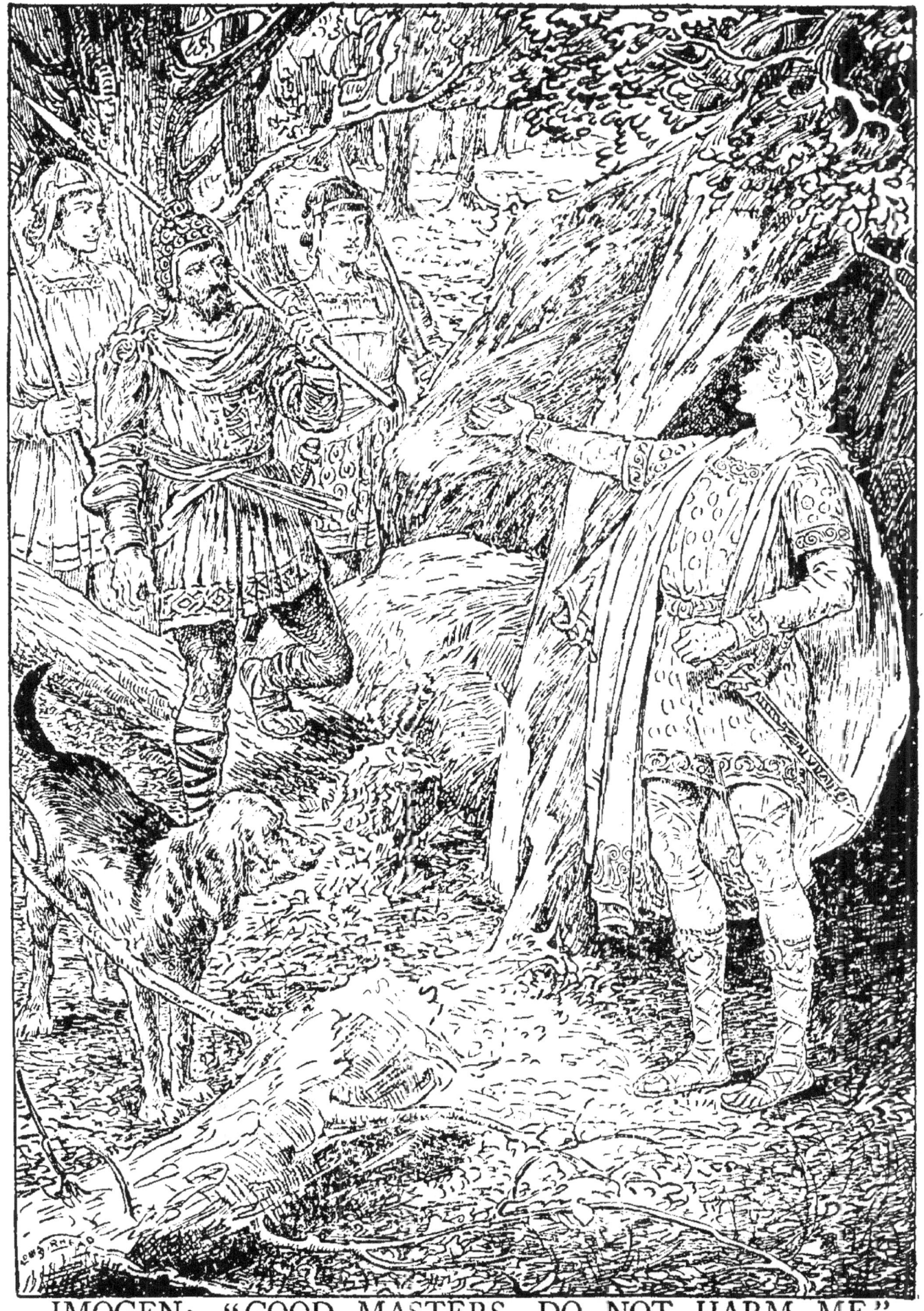

IMOGEN: "GOOD MASTERS, DO NOT HARM ME"

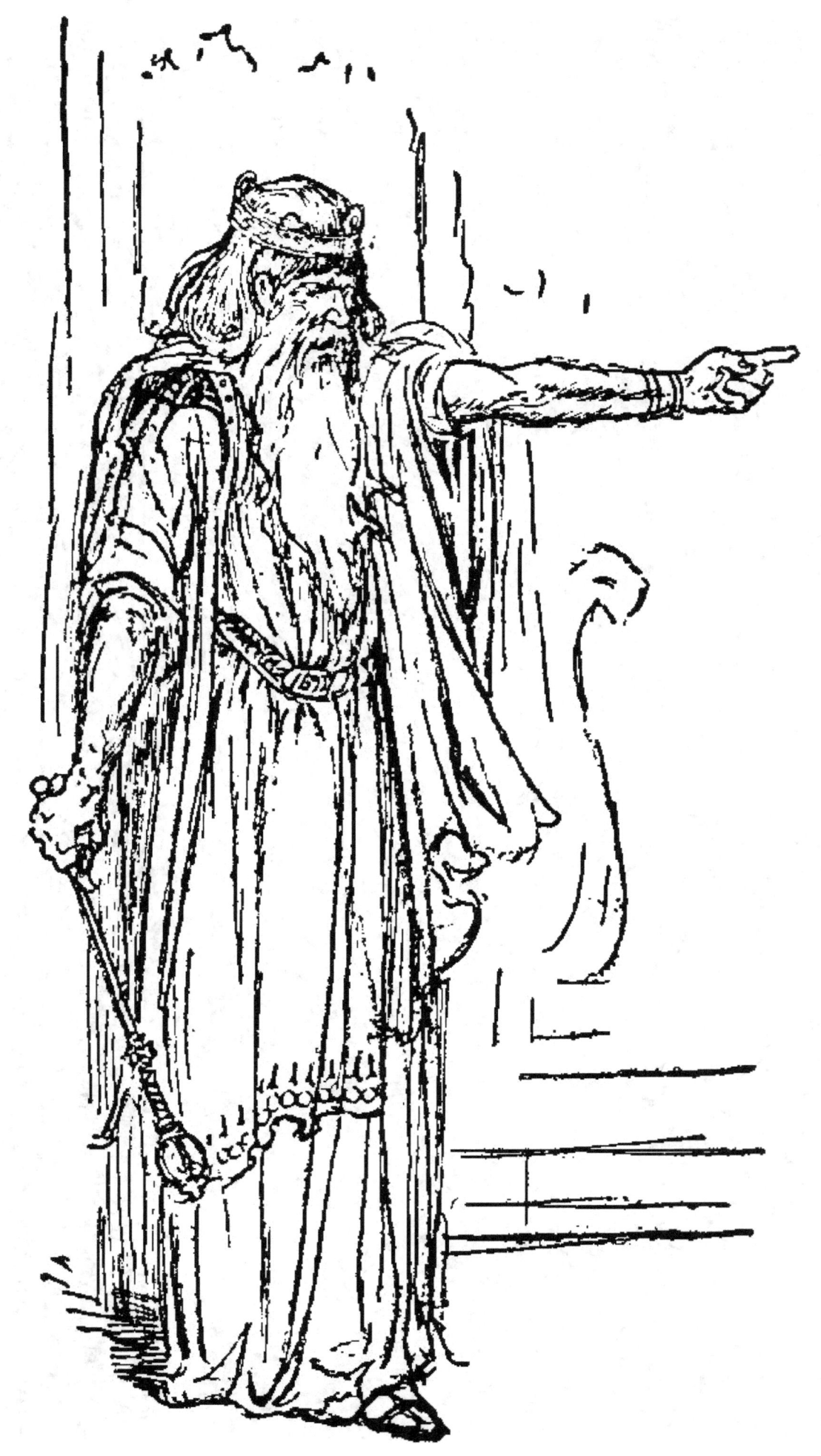

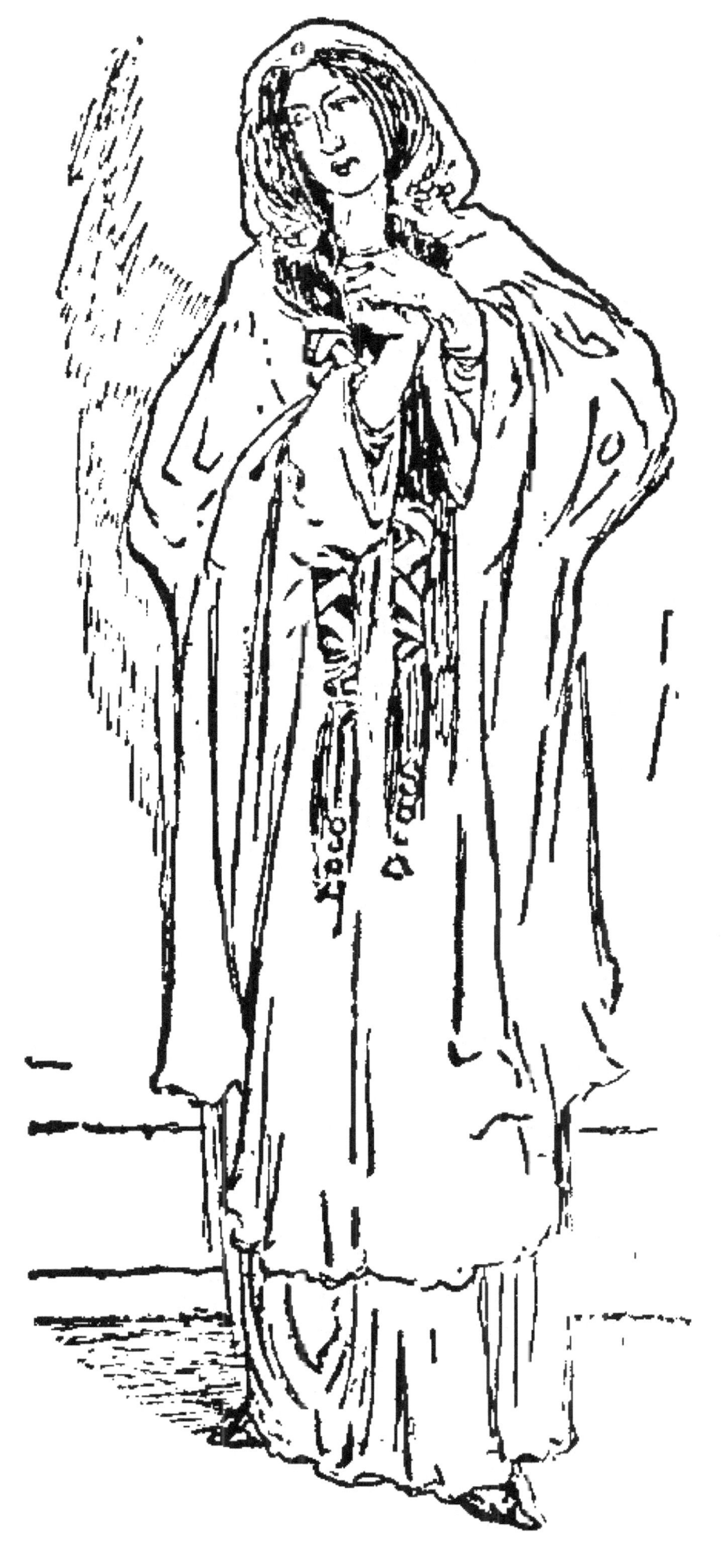

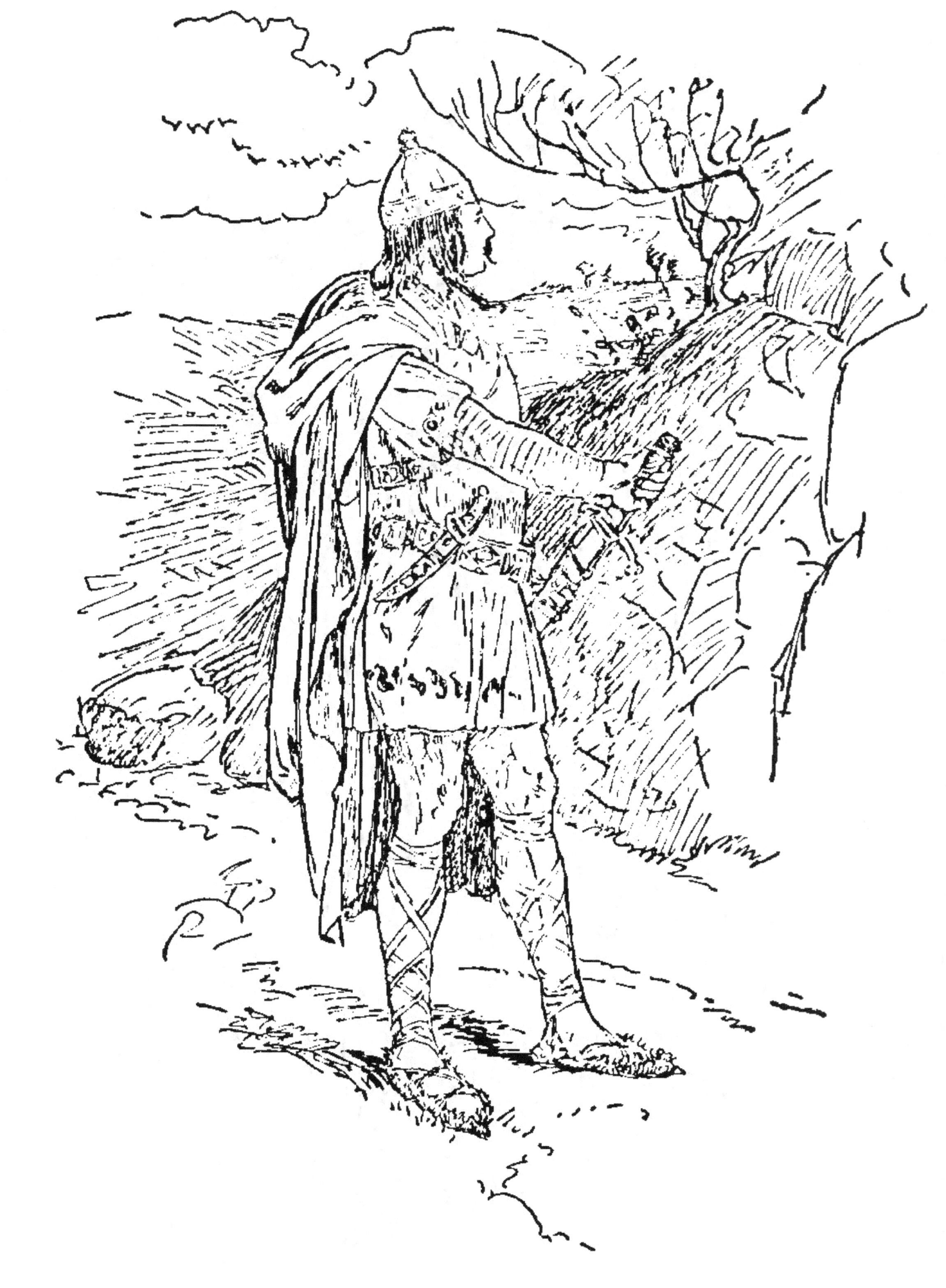

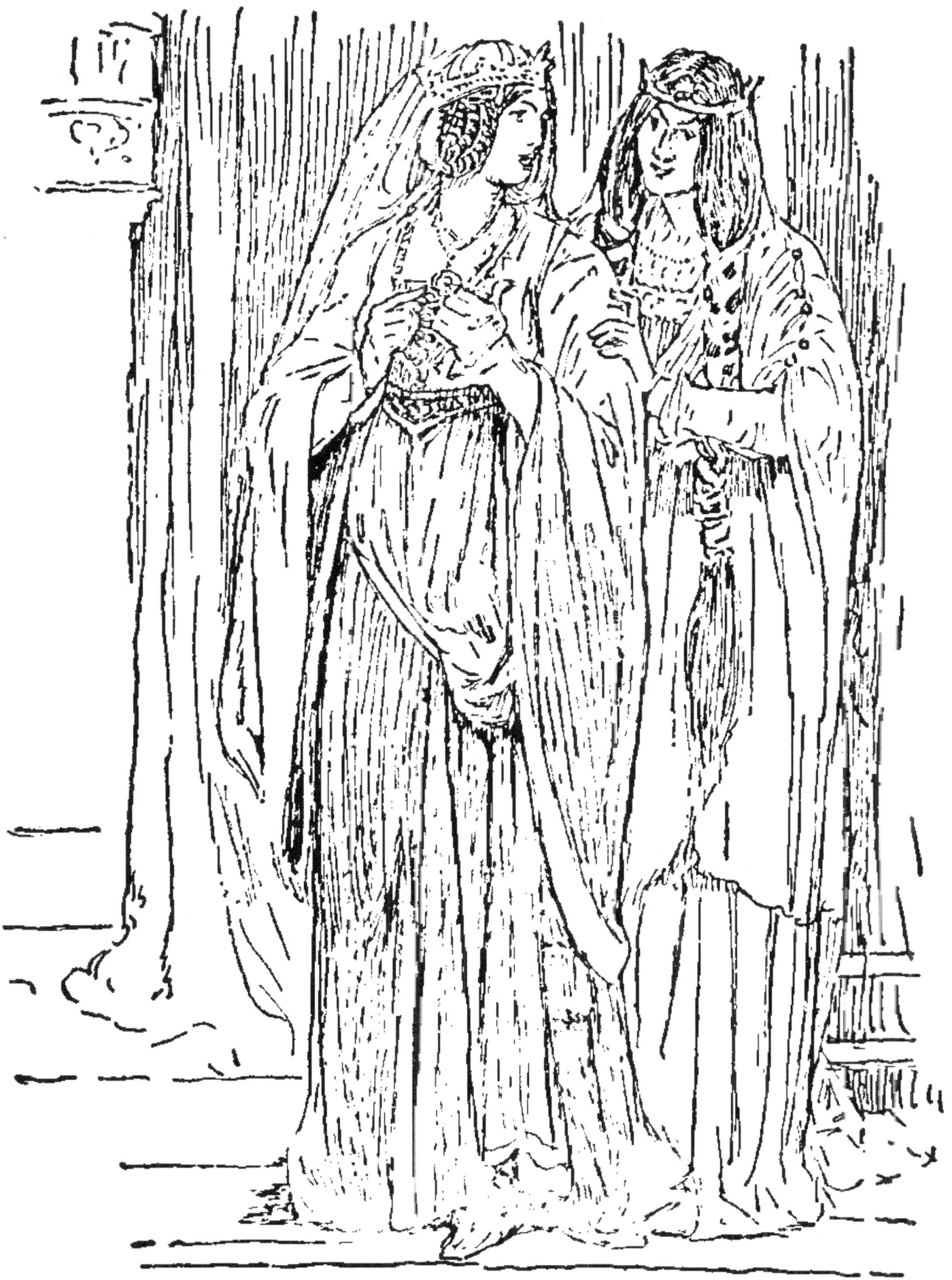

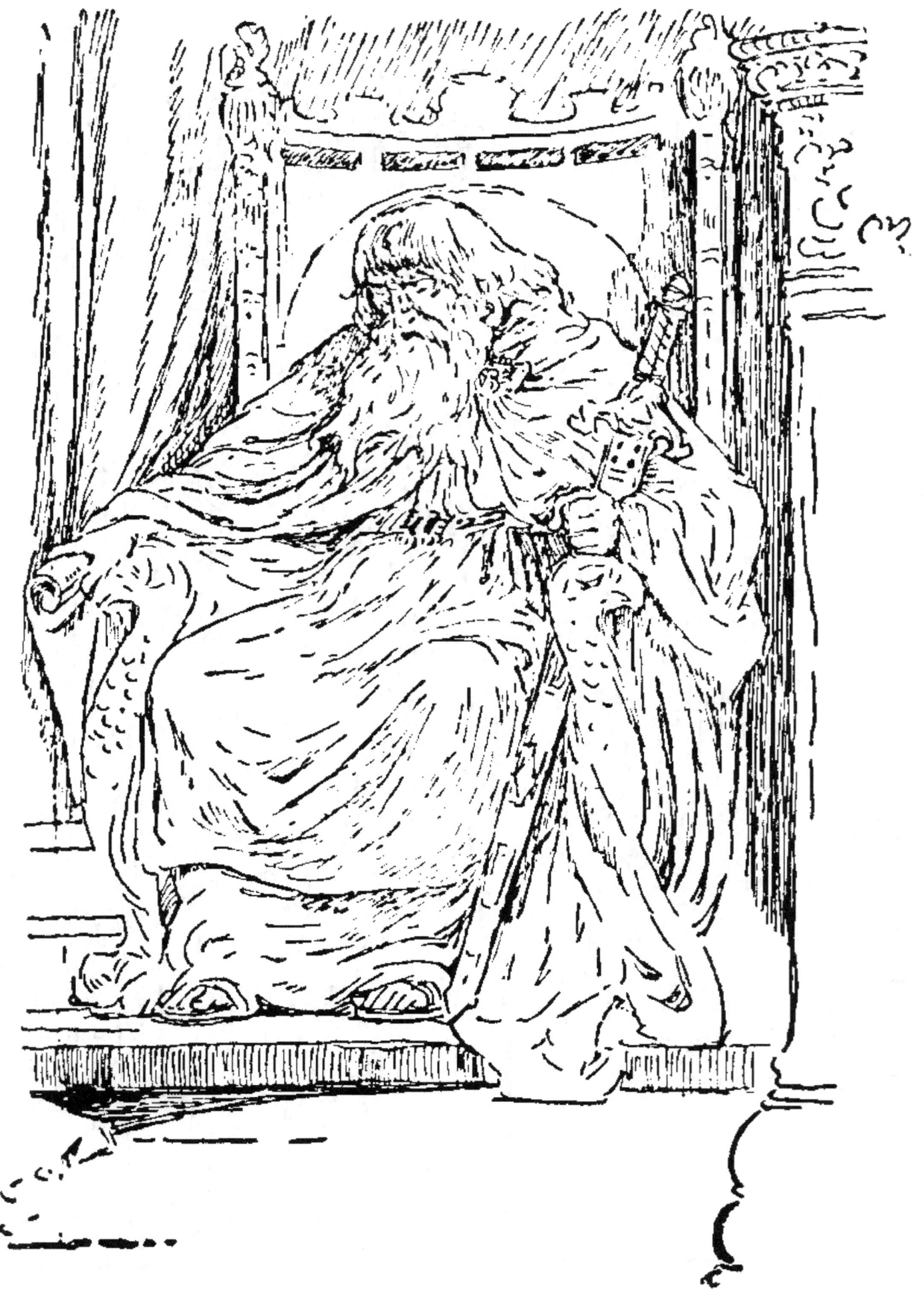

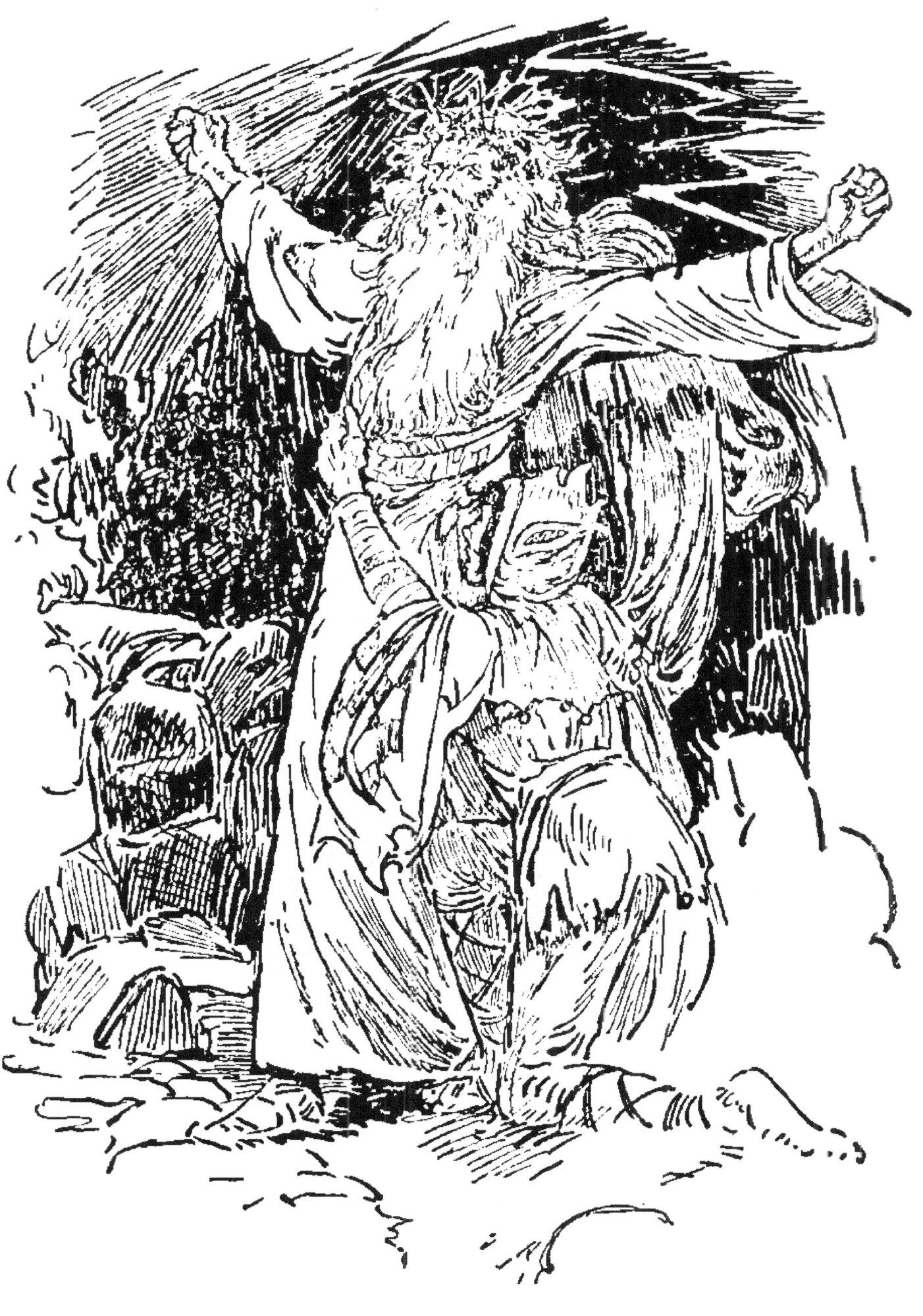

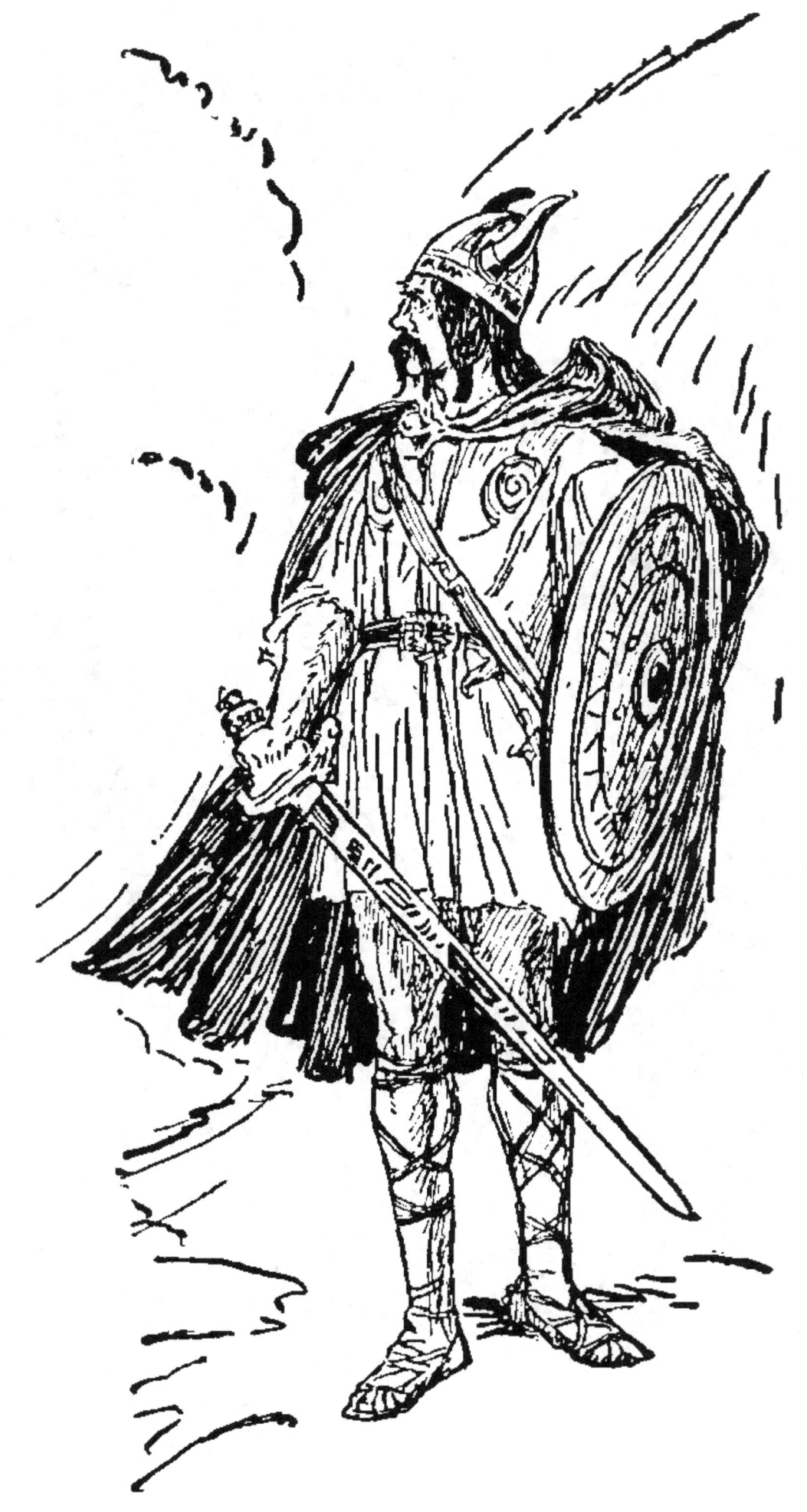

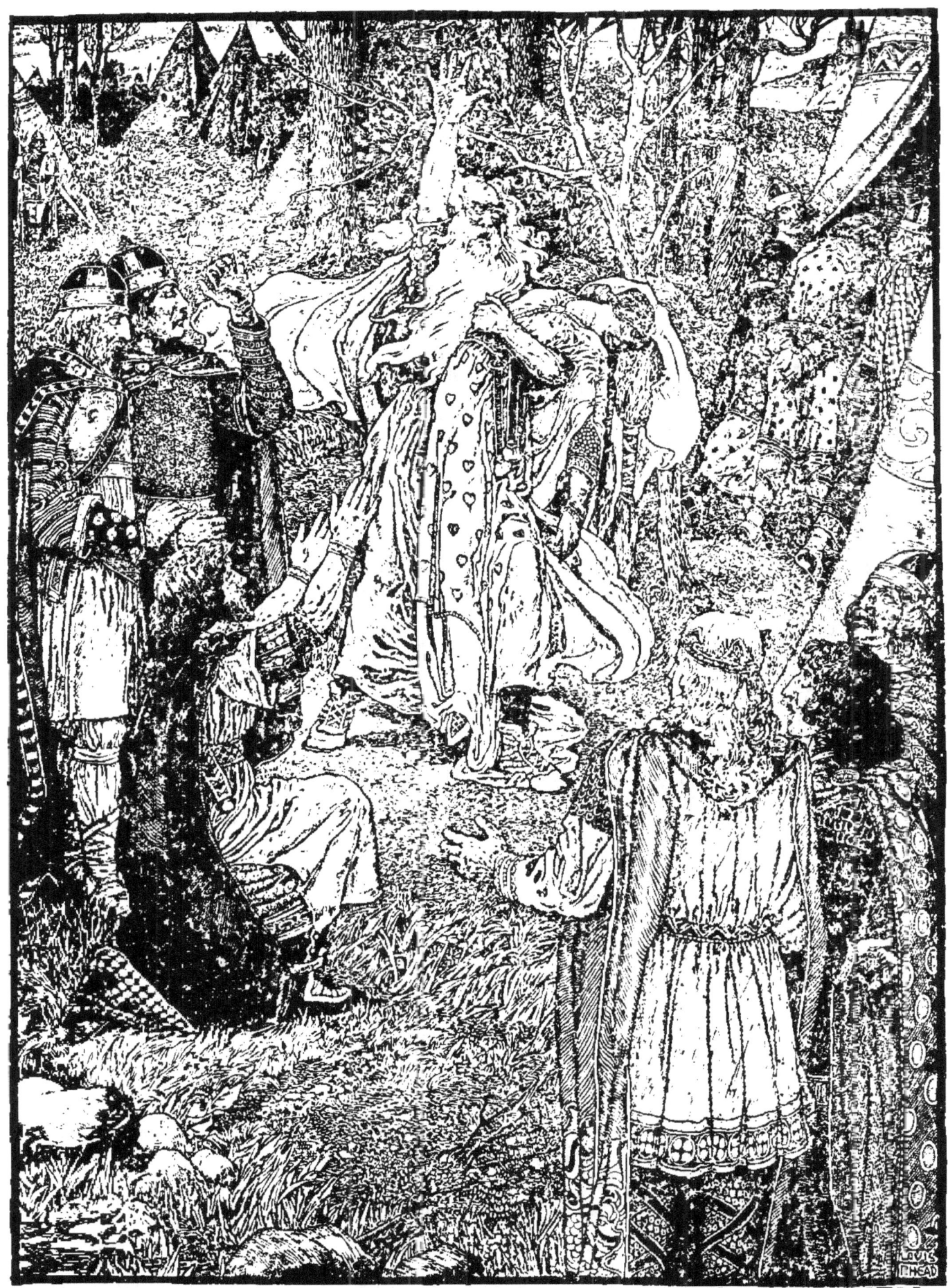

"HOWL, HOWL, HOWL, HOWL! O, YOU ARE MEN OF STONES"

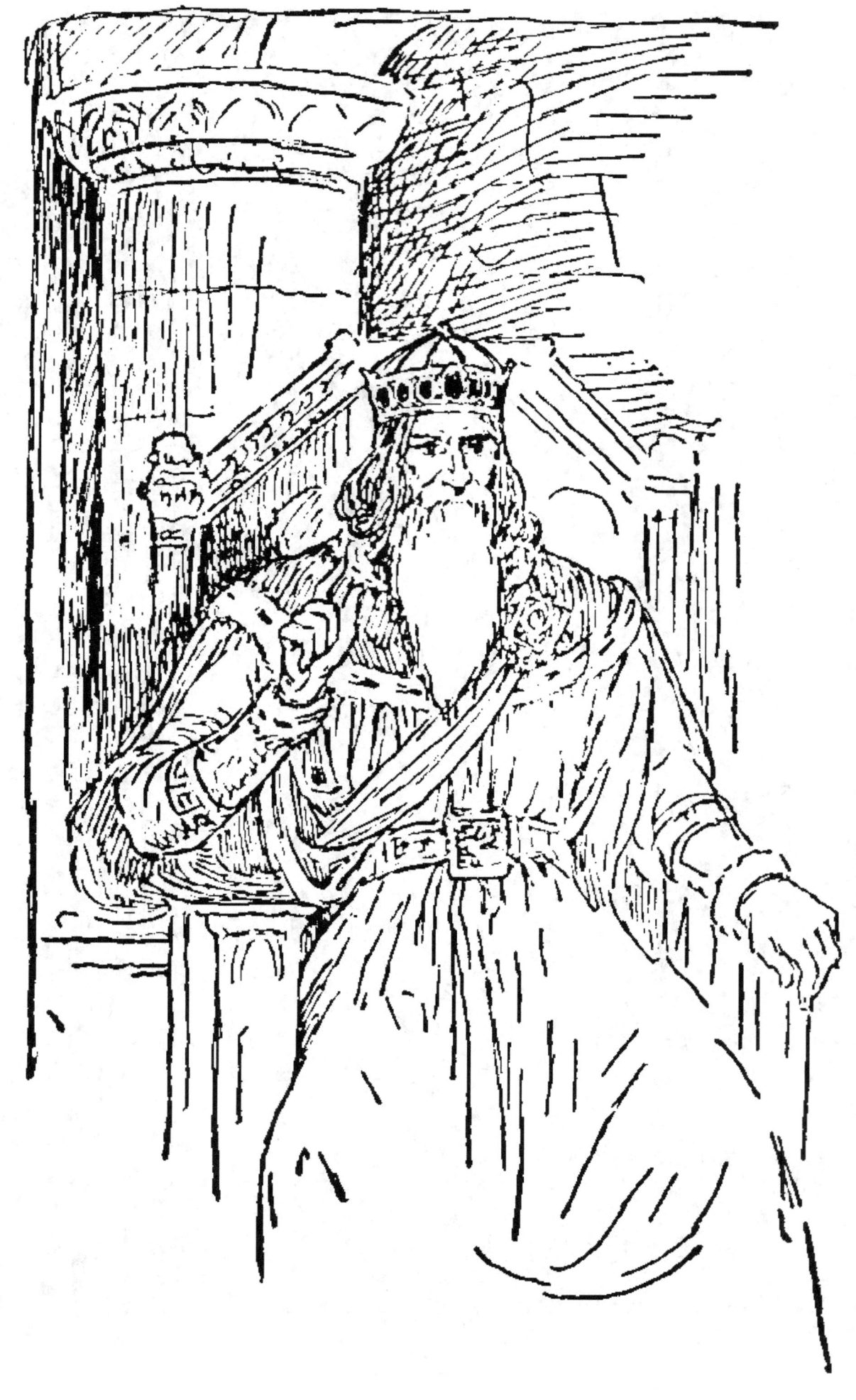

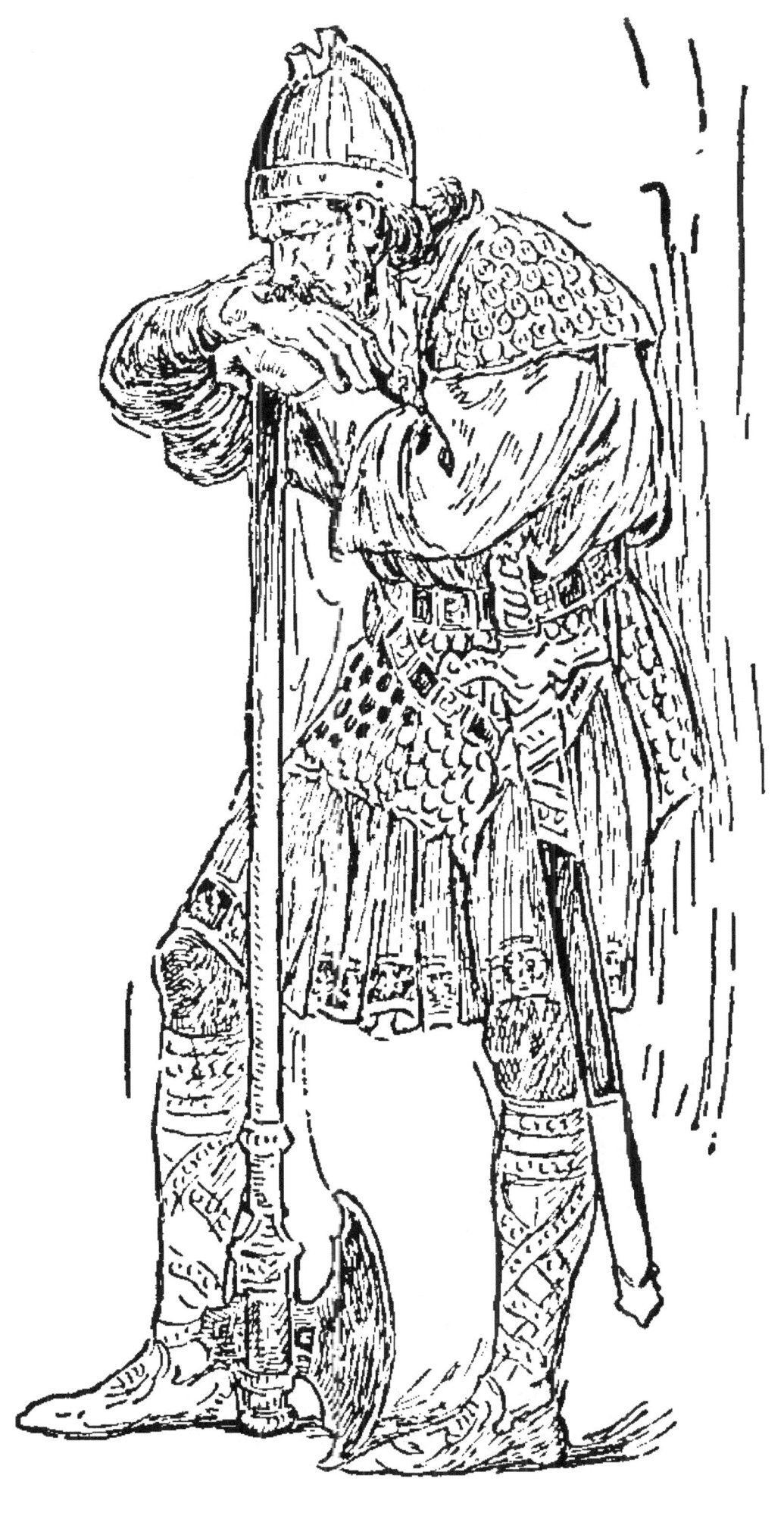

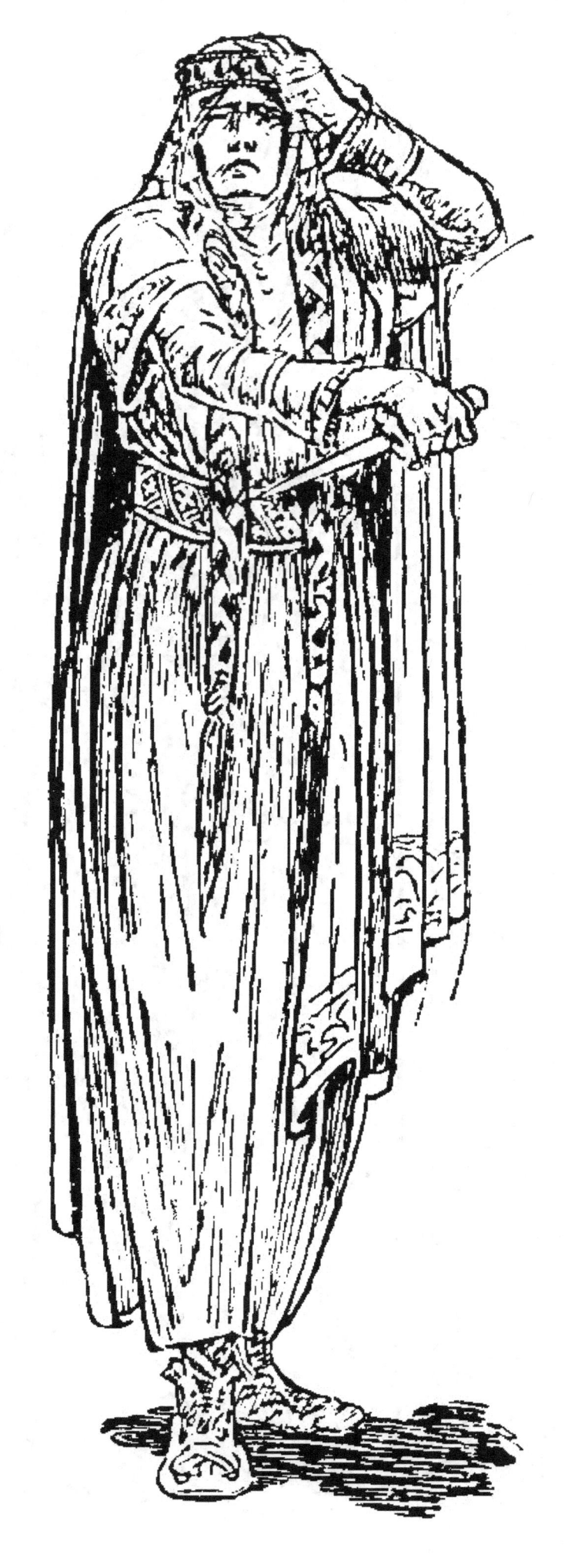

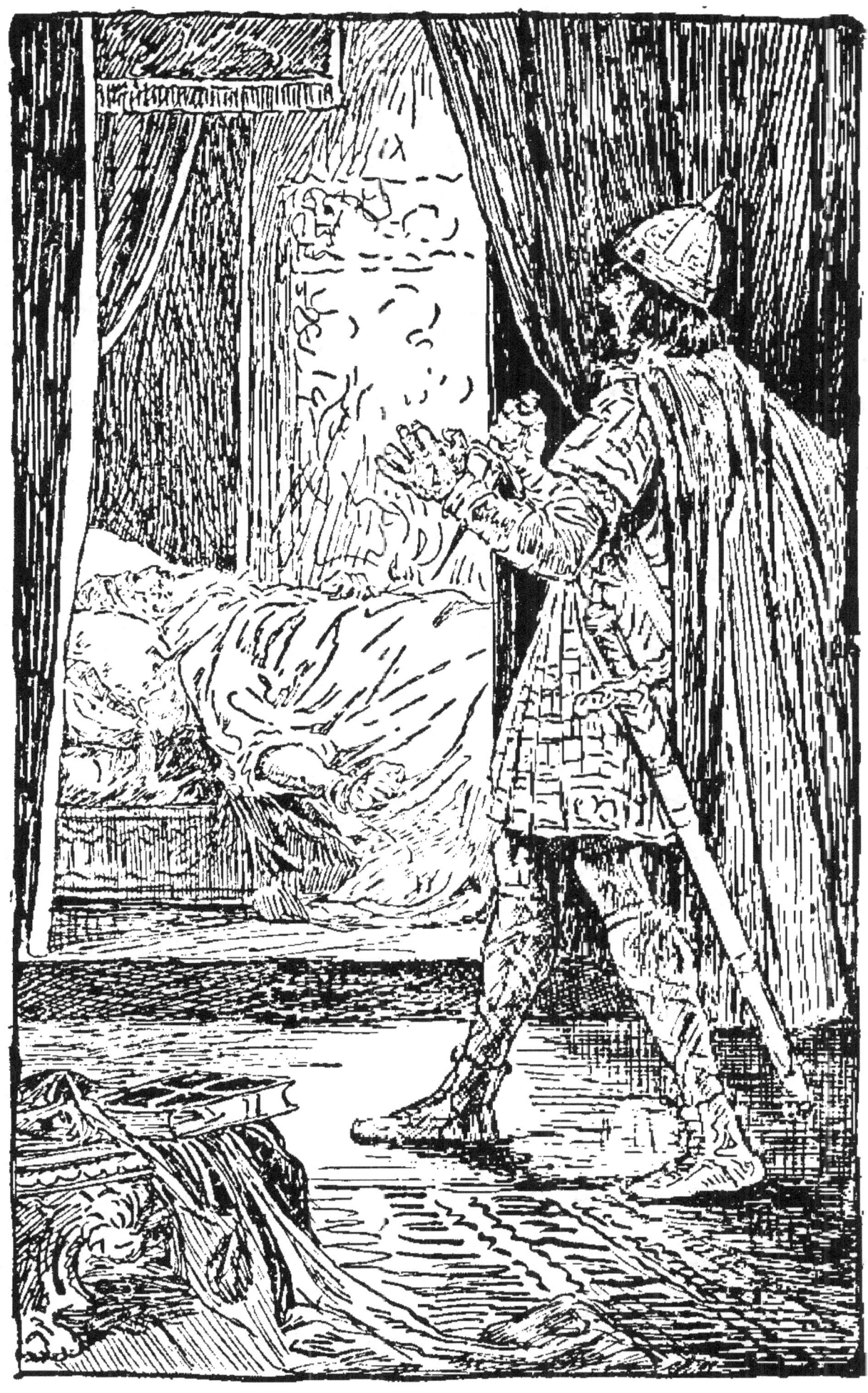

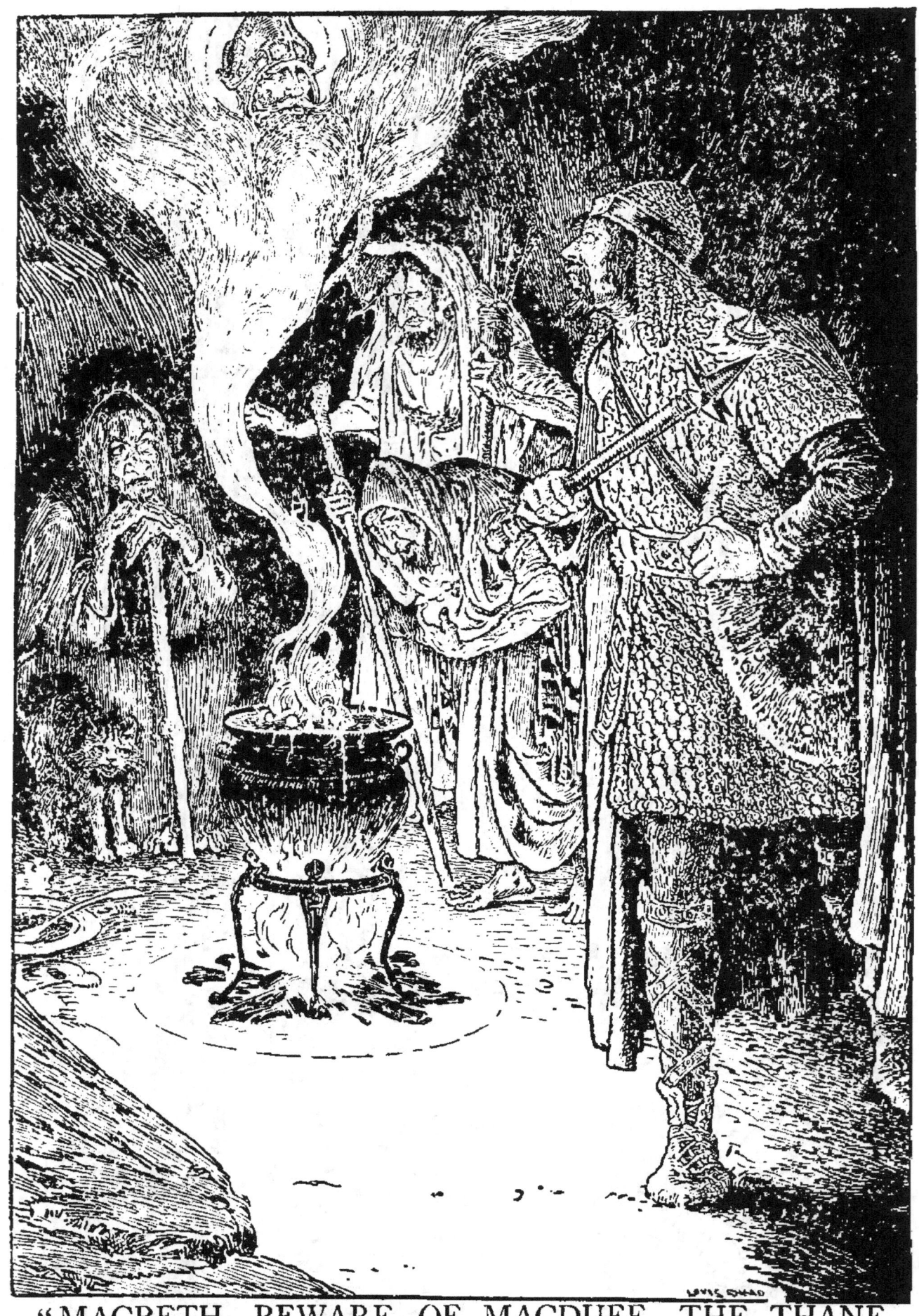

"MACBETH, BEWARE OF MACDUFF, THE THANE OF FIFE!"

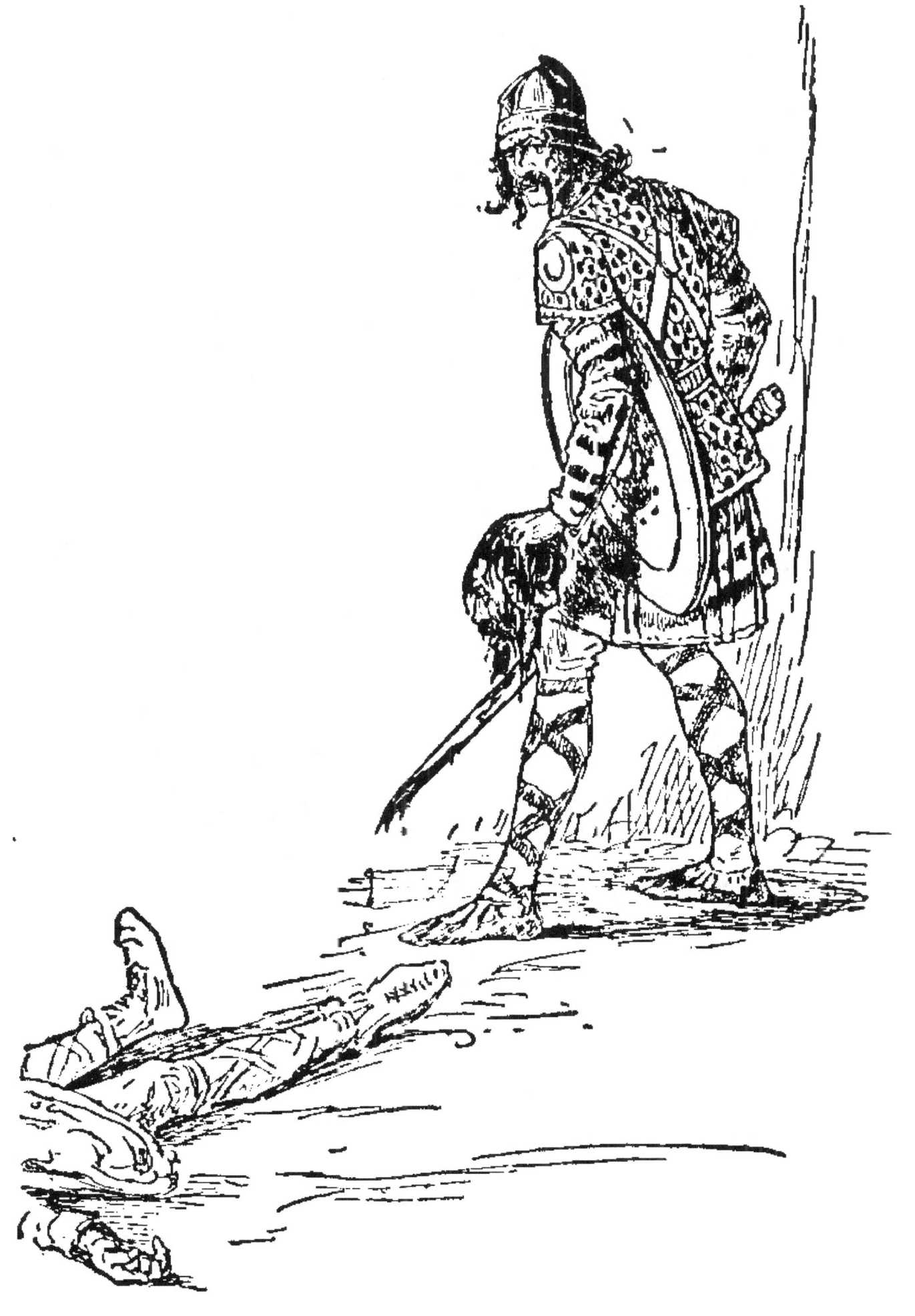

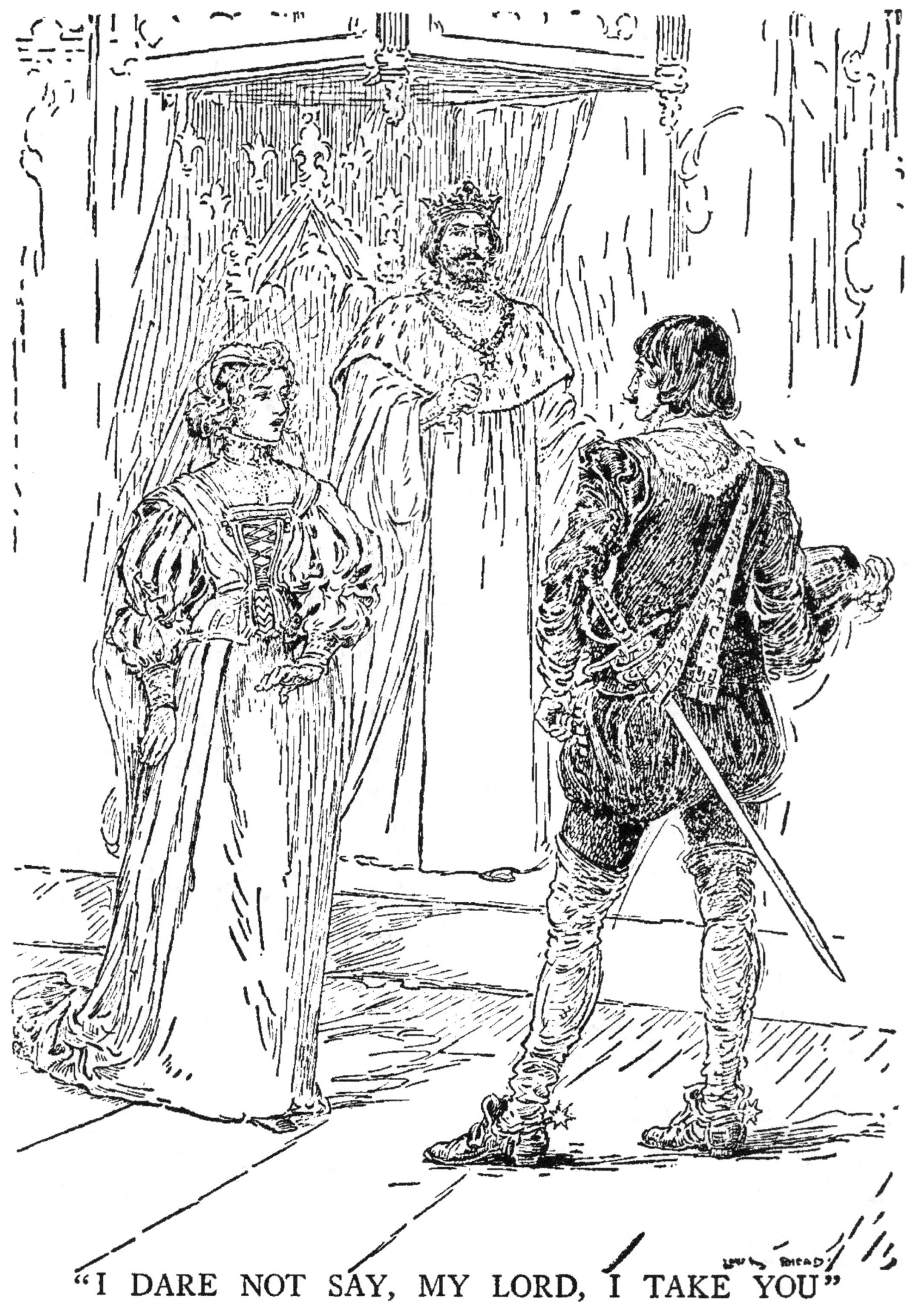

"I DARE NOT SAY, MY LORD, I TAKE YOU"

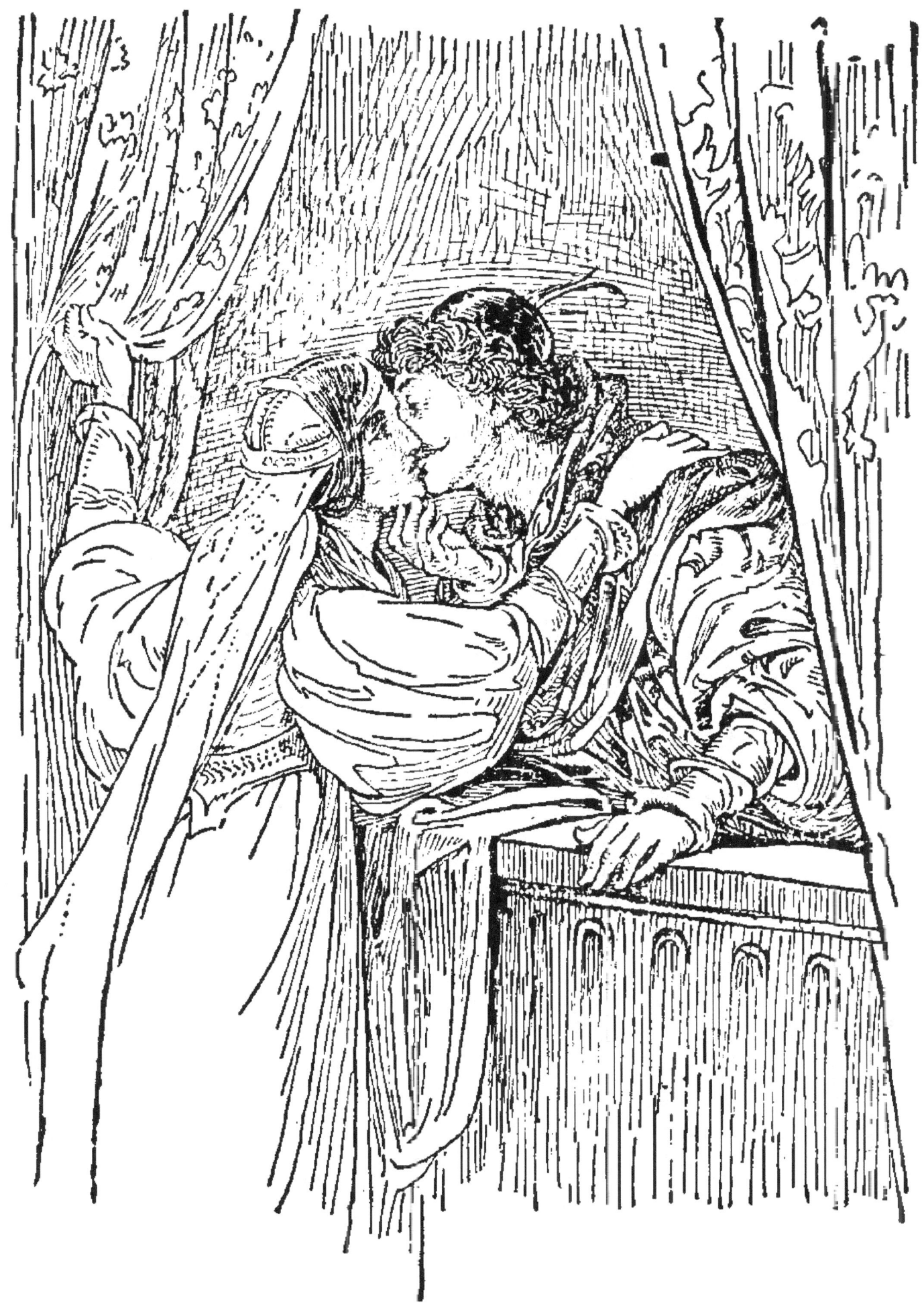

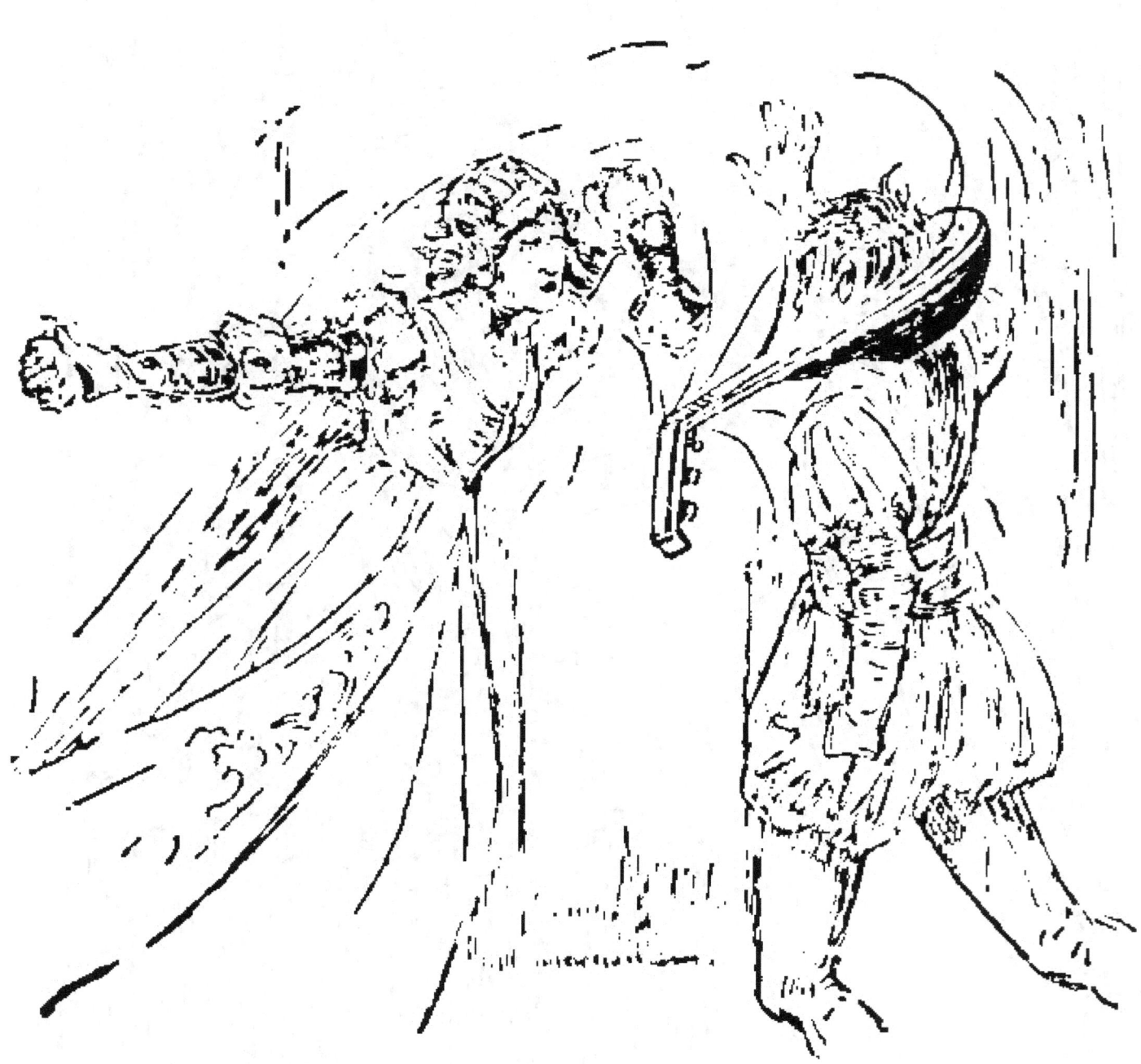

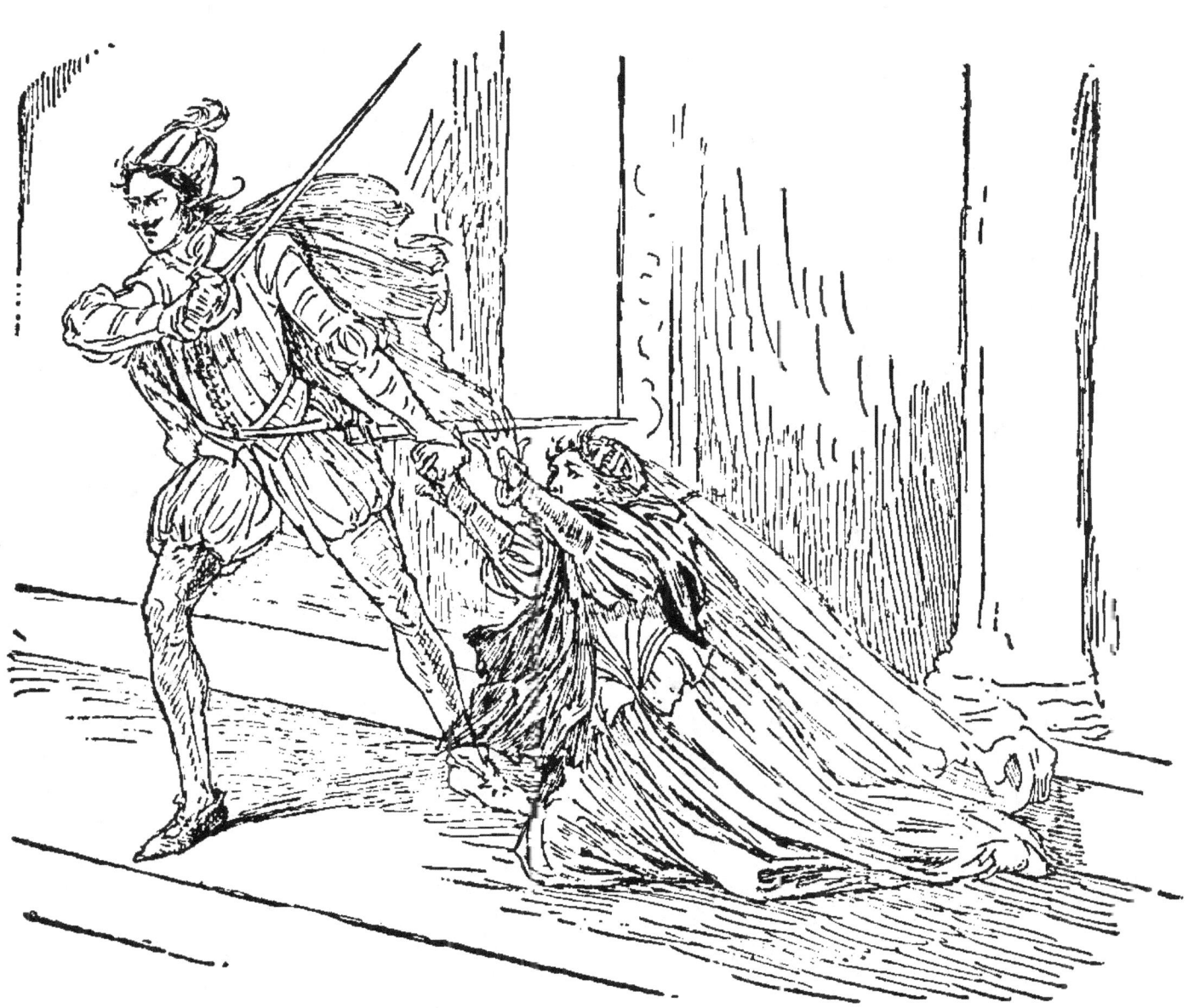

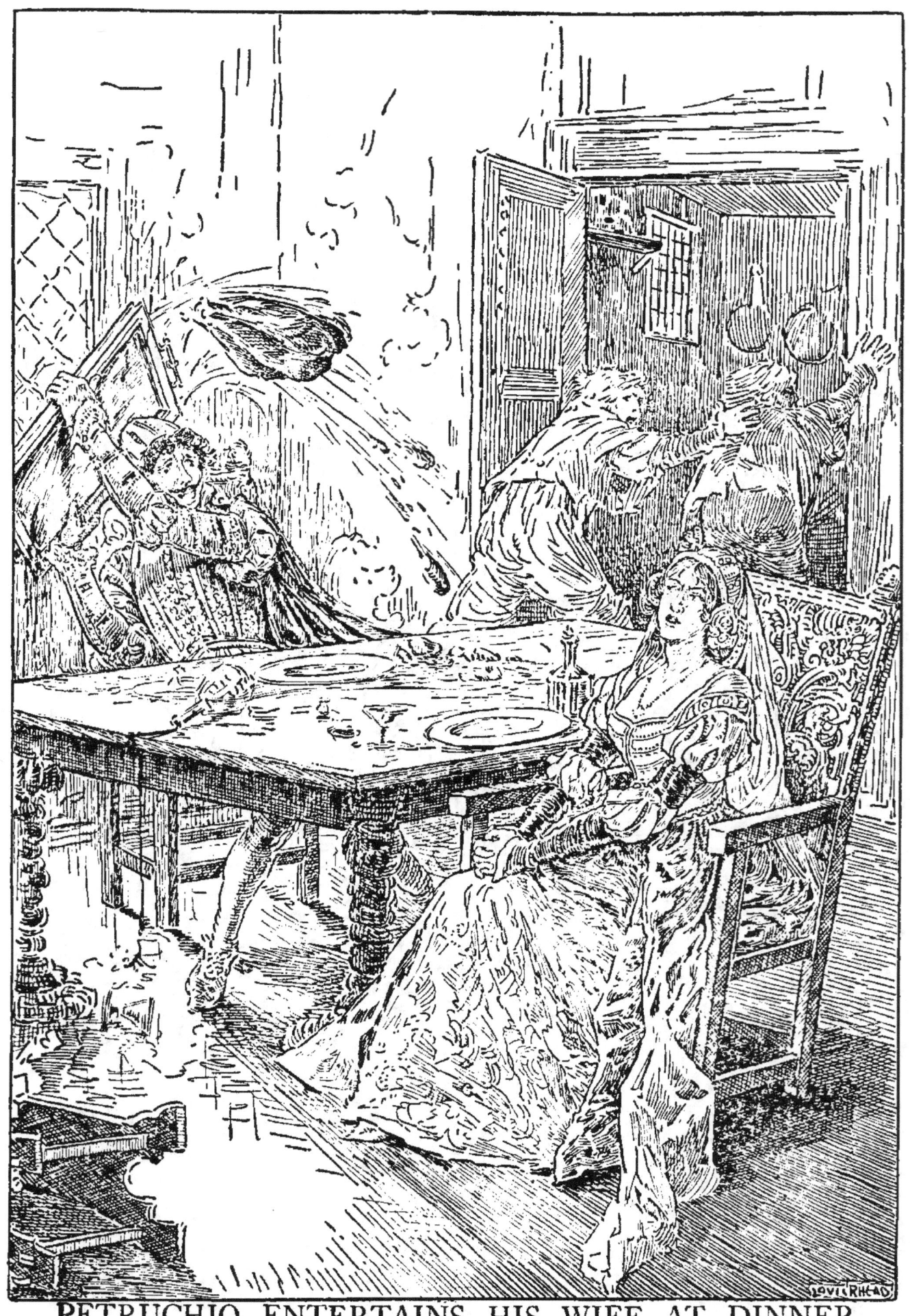
PETRUCHIO ENTERTAINS HIS WIFE AT DINNER

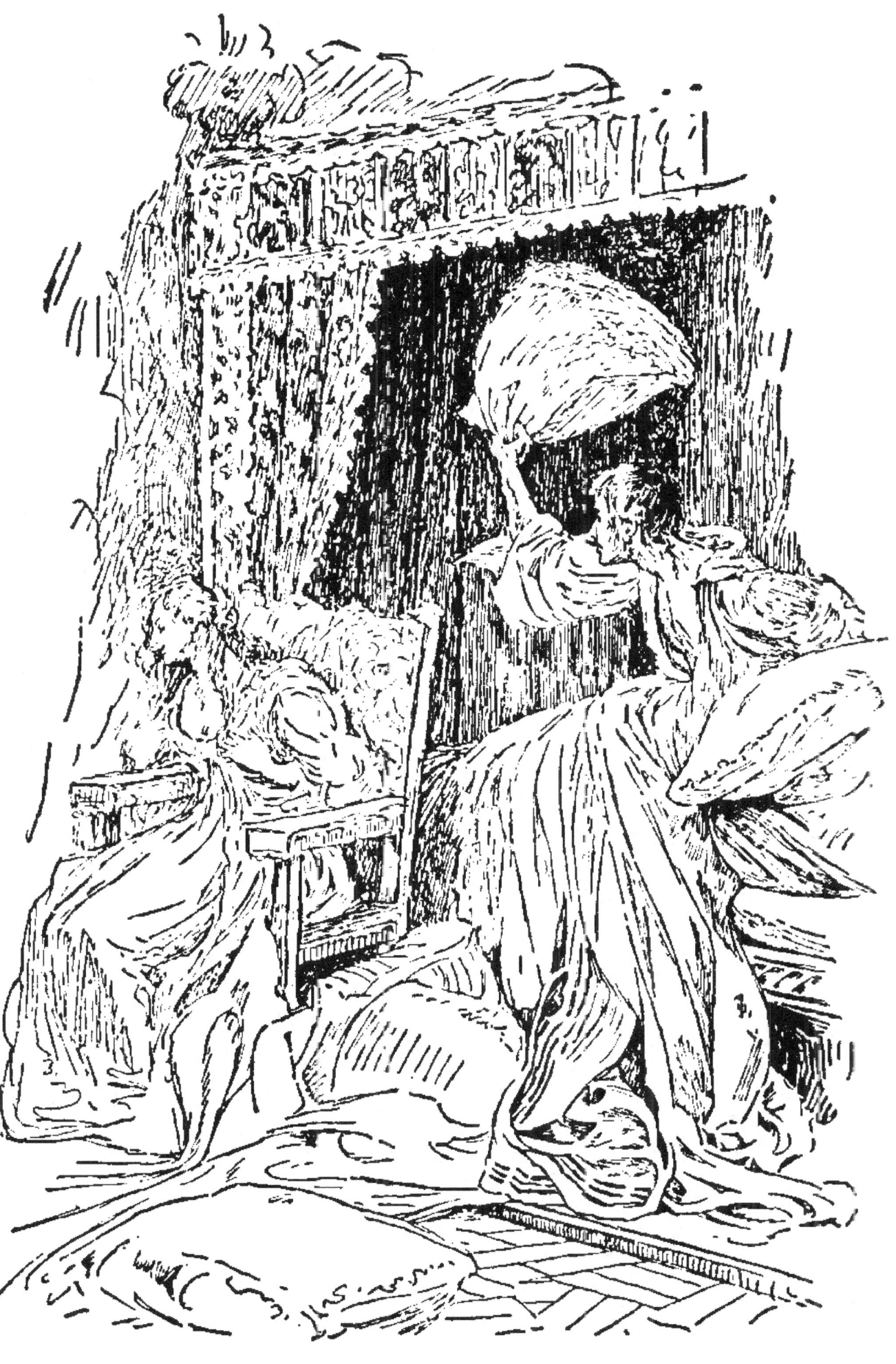

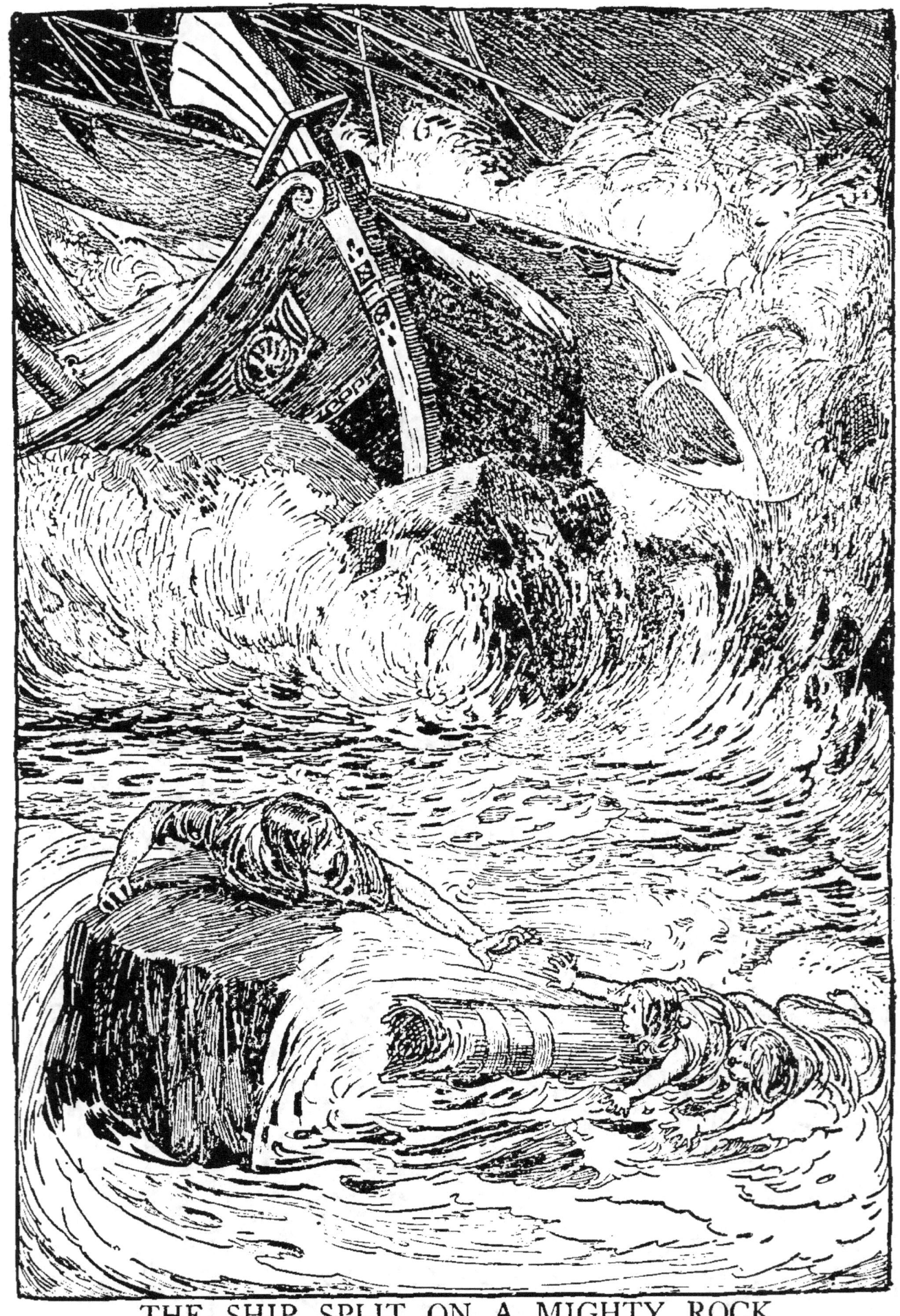

THE SHIP SPLIT ON A MIGHTY ROCK

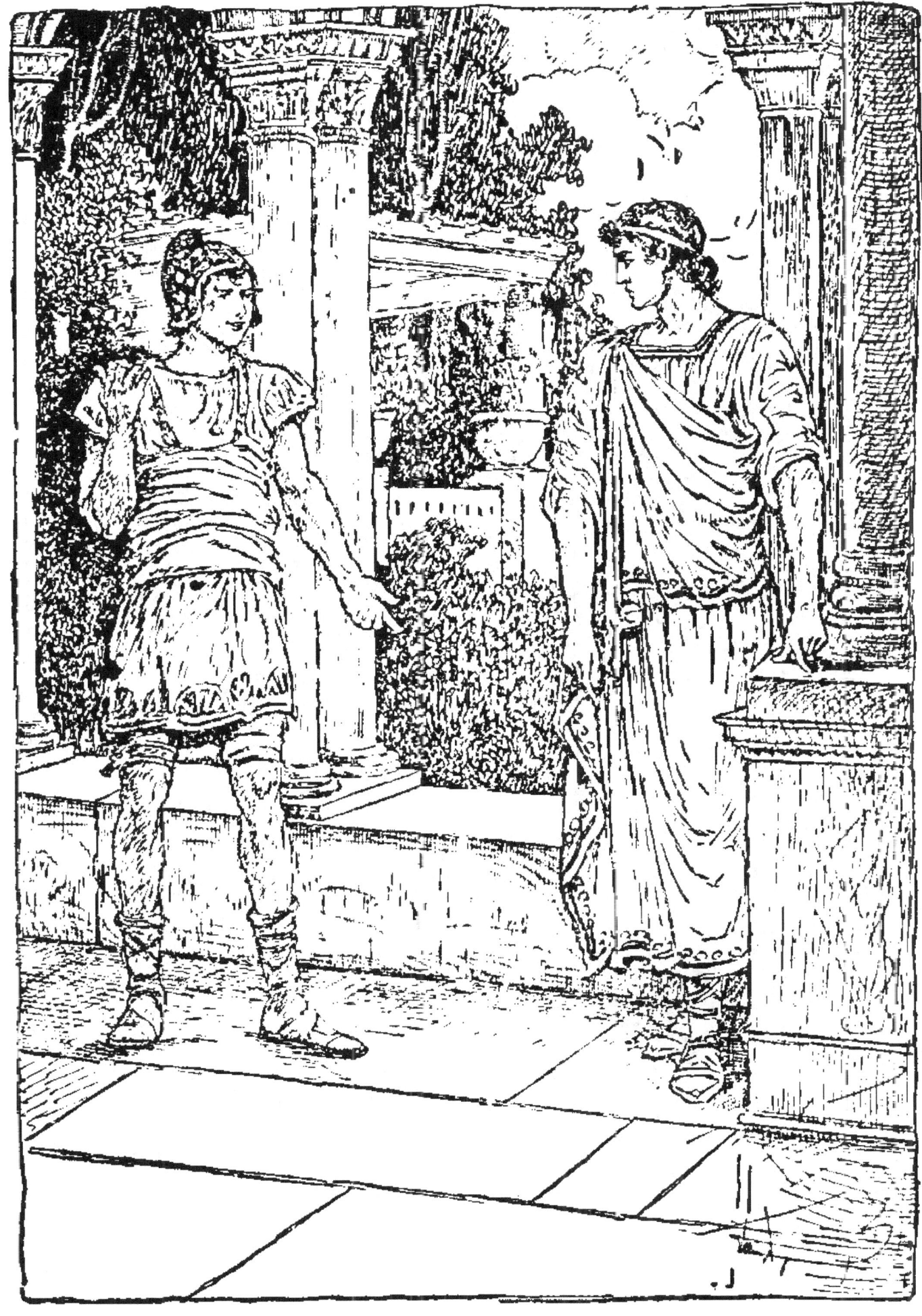

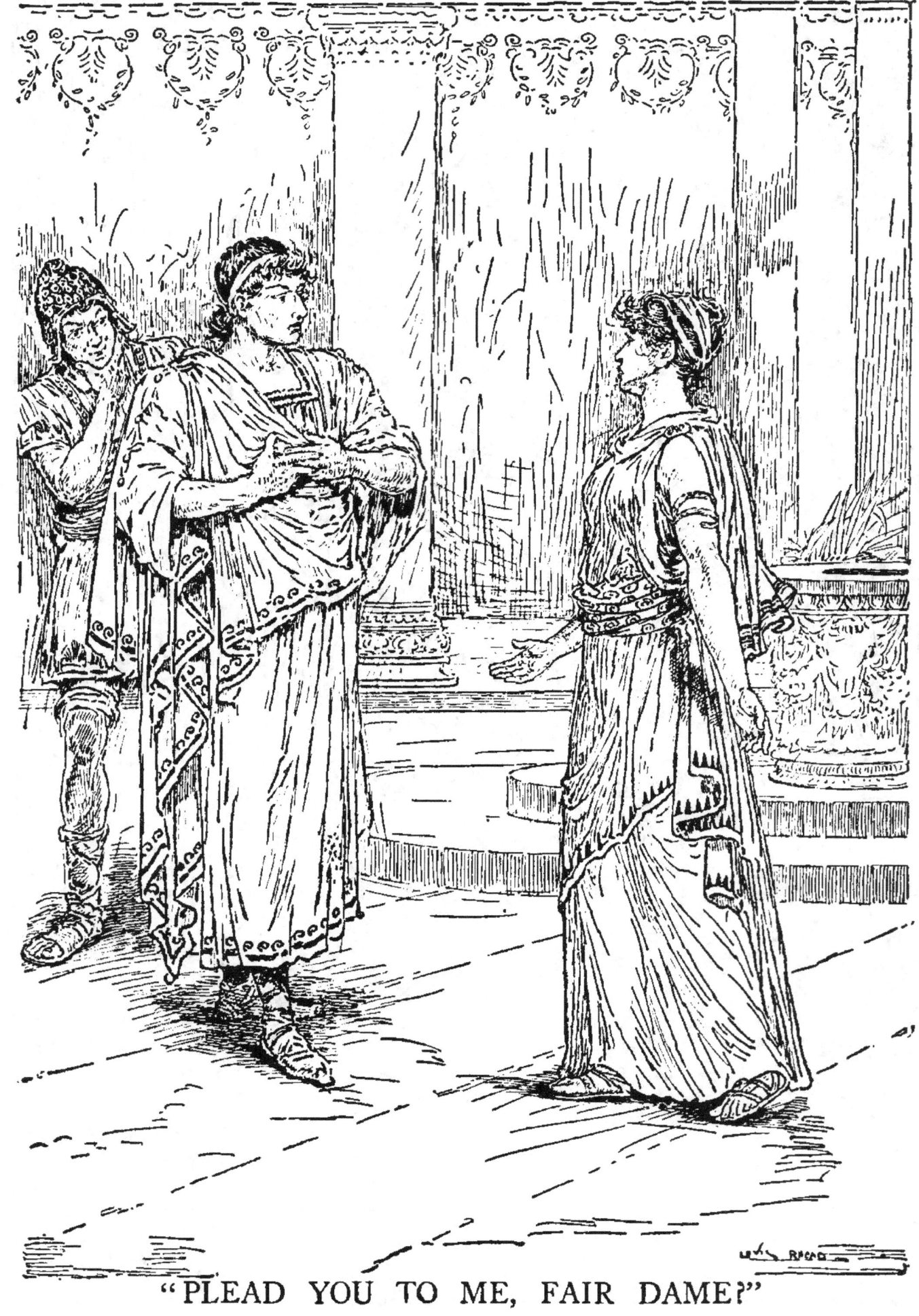

"PLEAD YOU TO ME, FAIR DAME?"

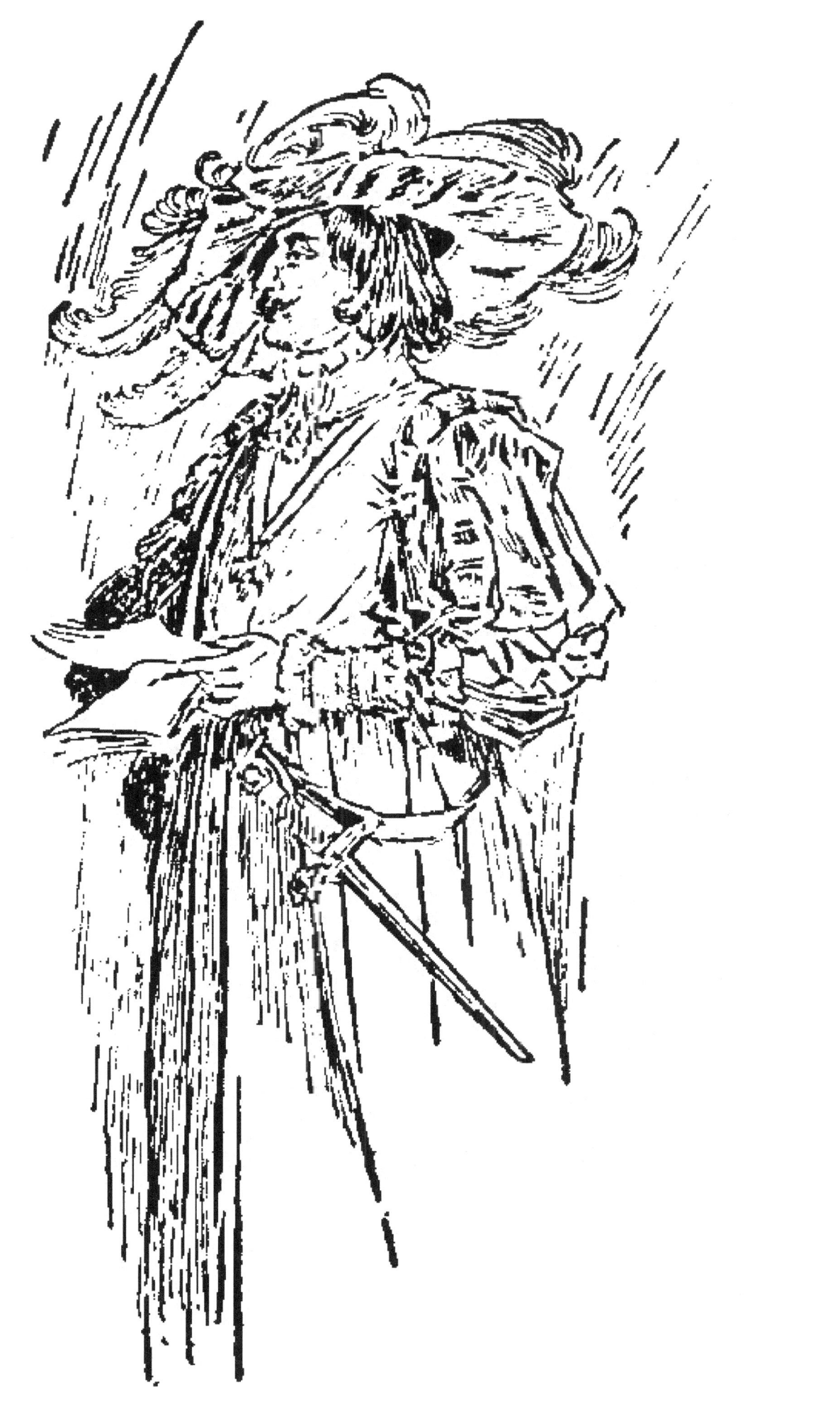

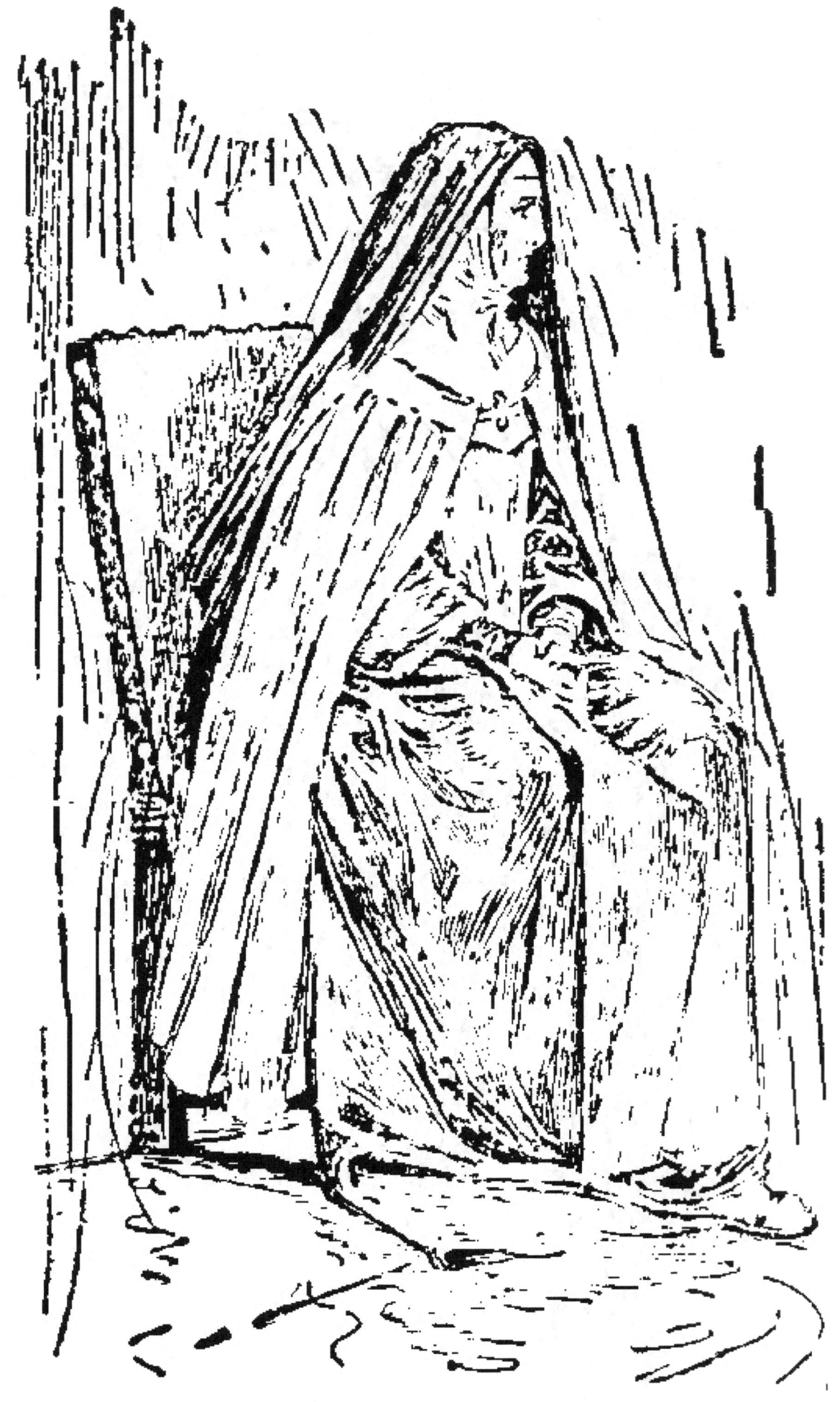

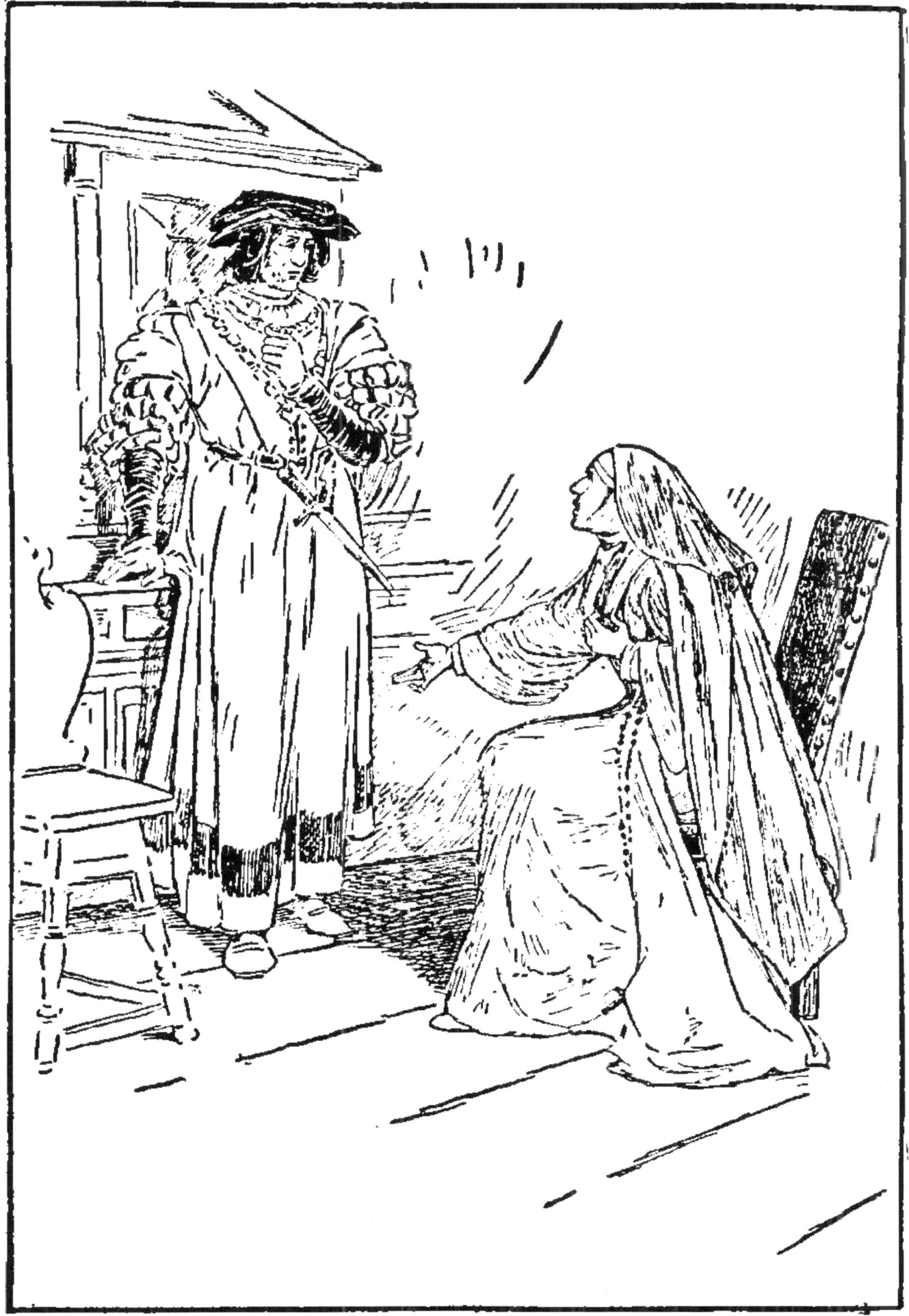

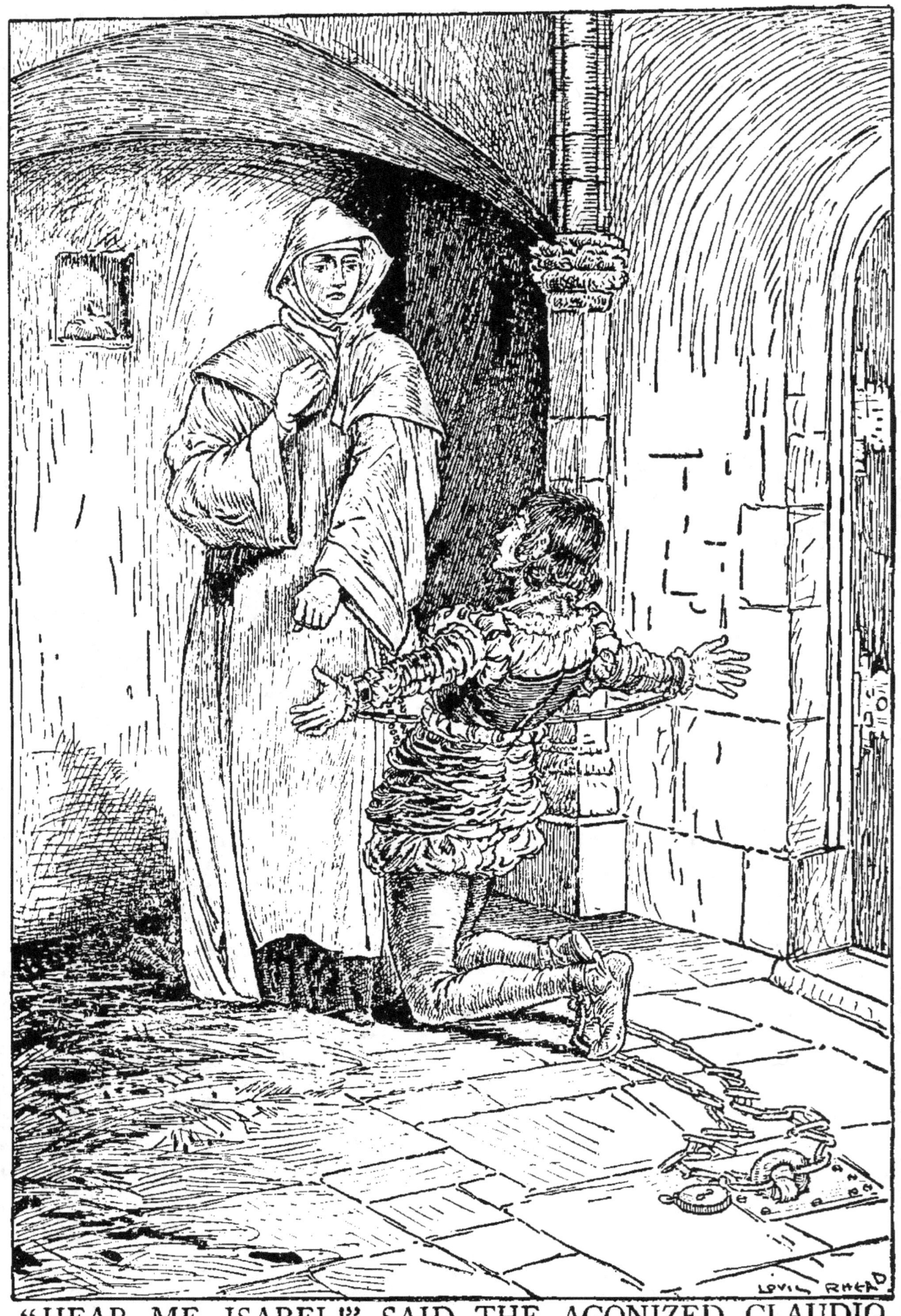
"HEAR ME, ISABEL!" SAID THE AGONIZED CLAUDIO

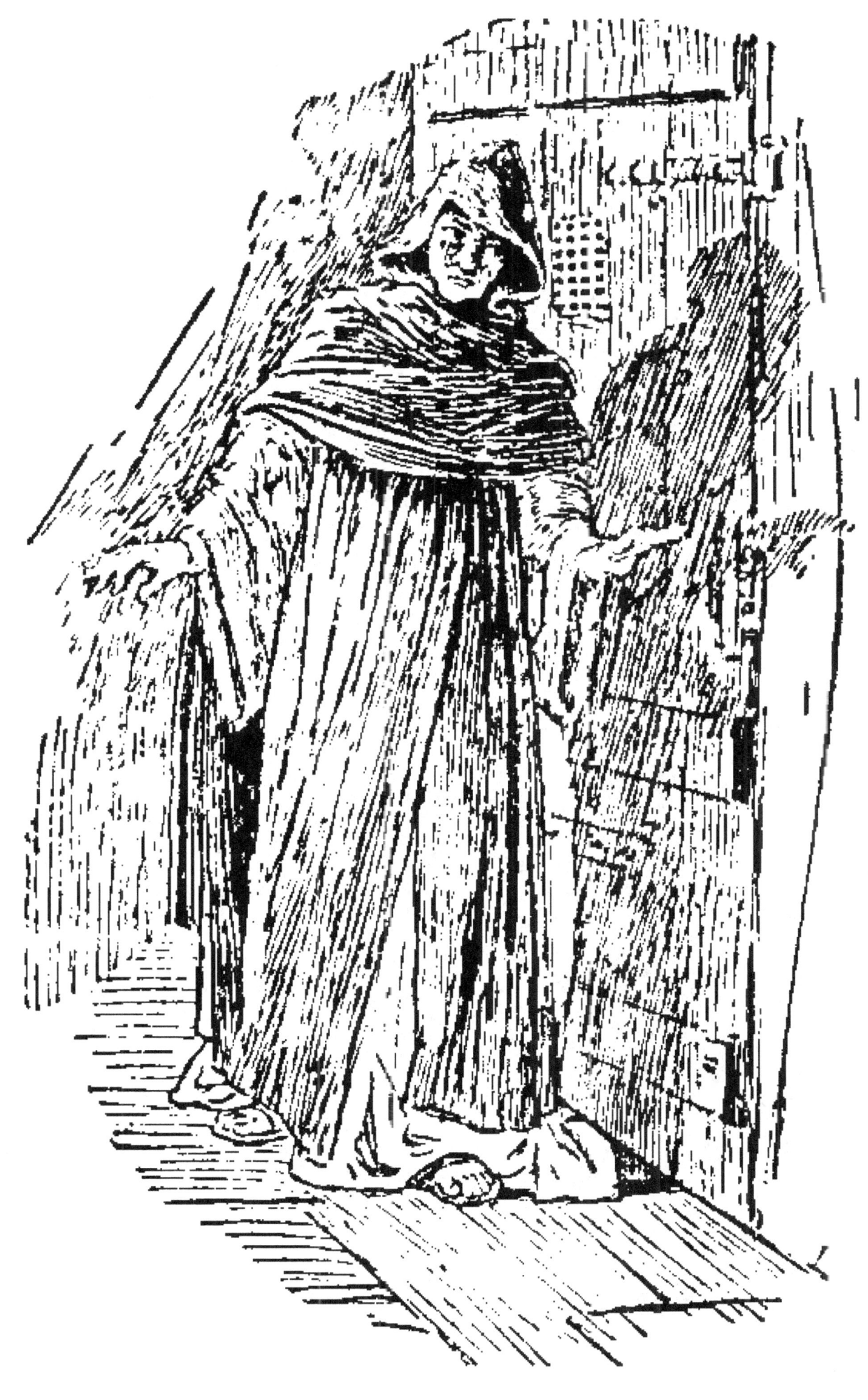

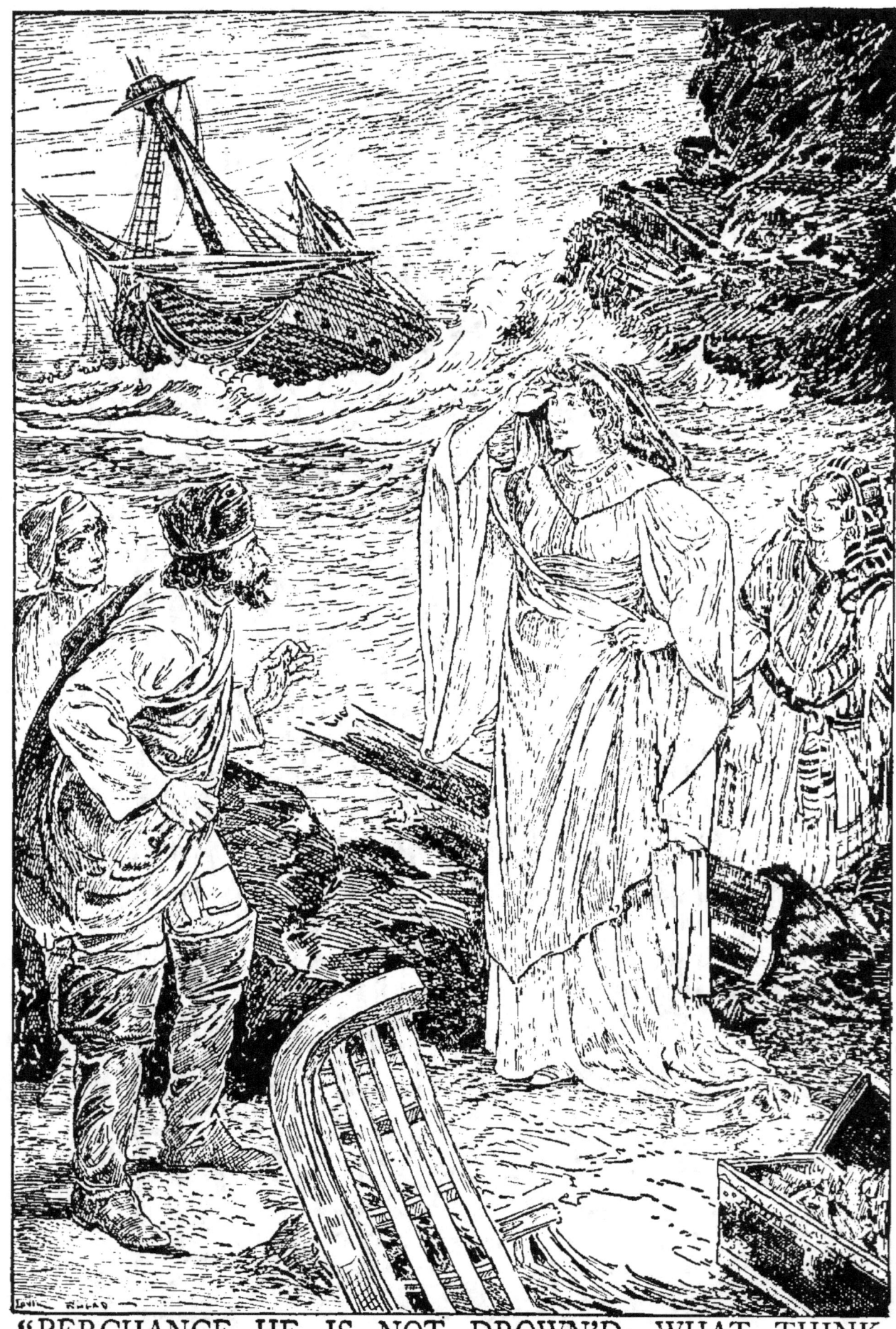

"PERCHANCE HE IS NOT DROWN'D; WHAT THINK YOU, CAPTAIN?"

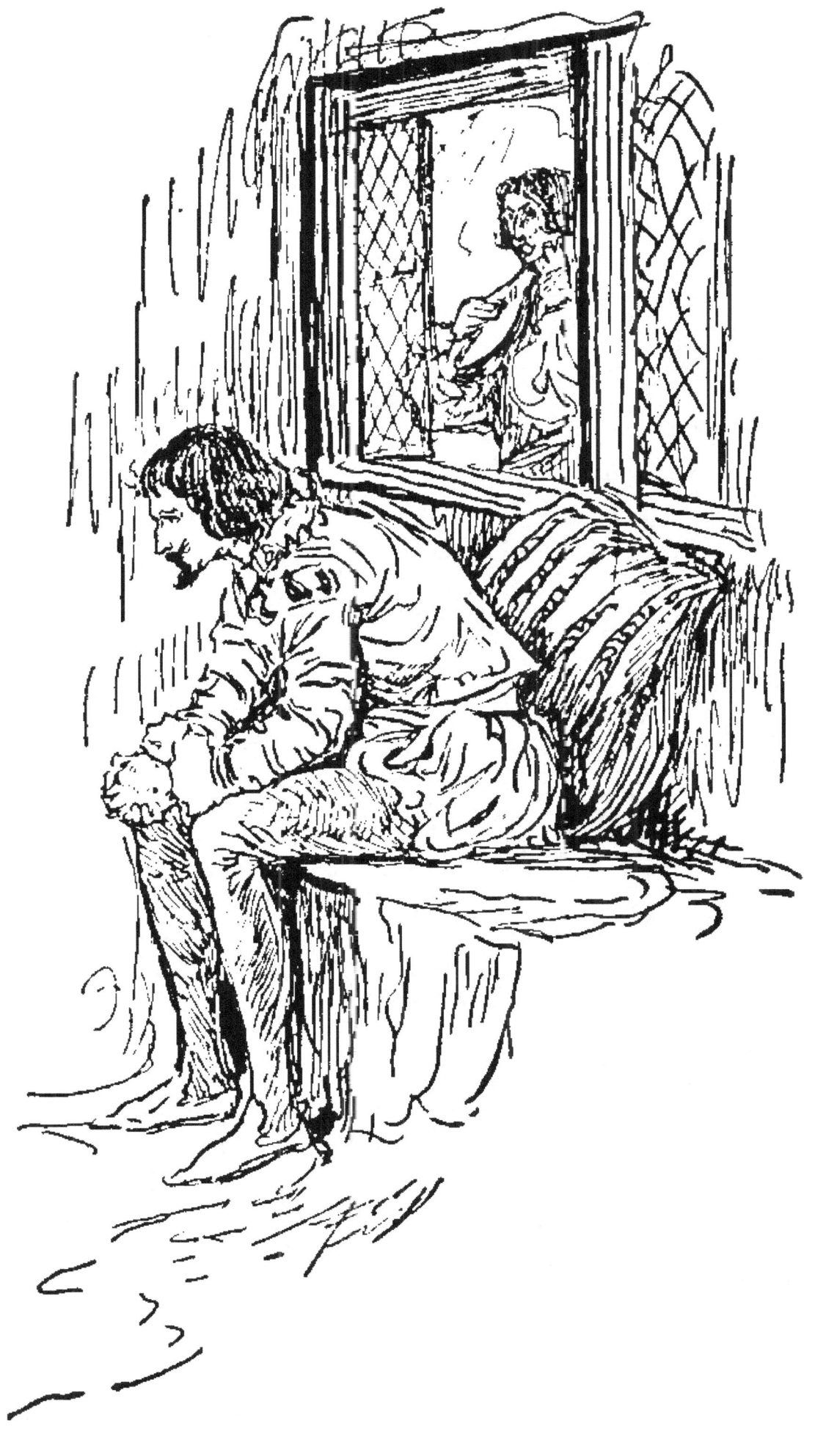

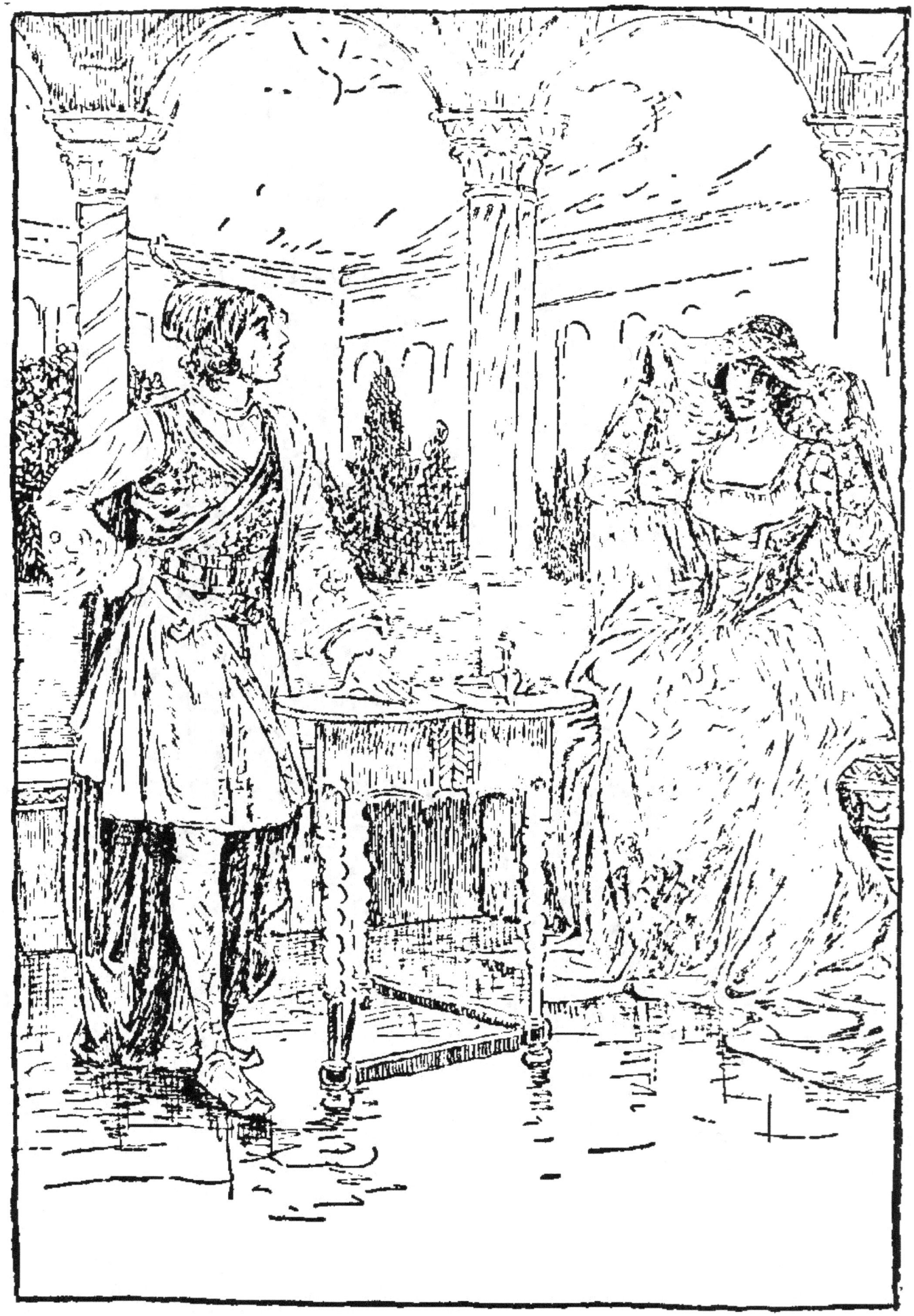

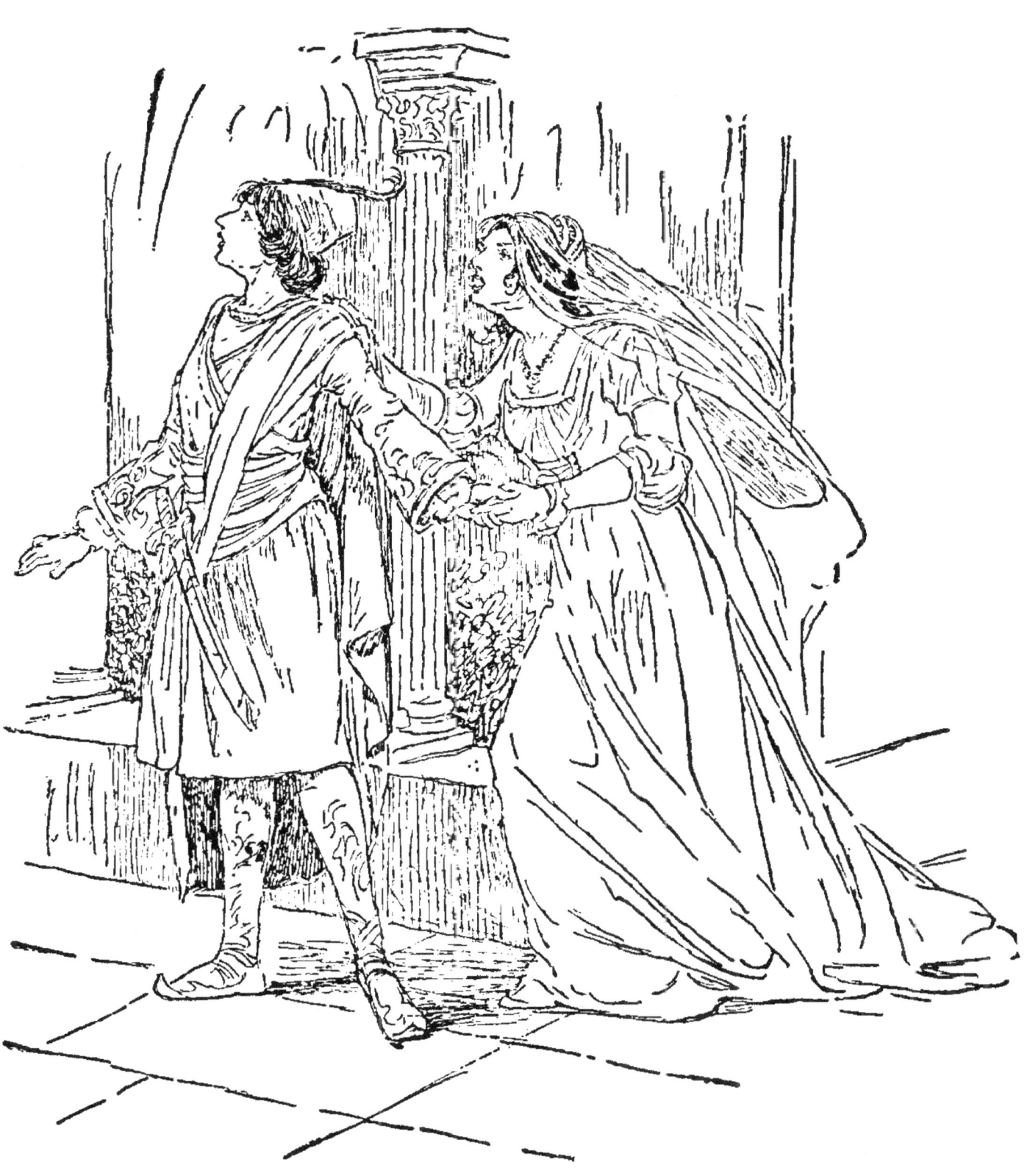

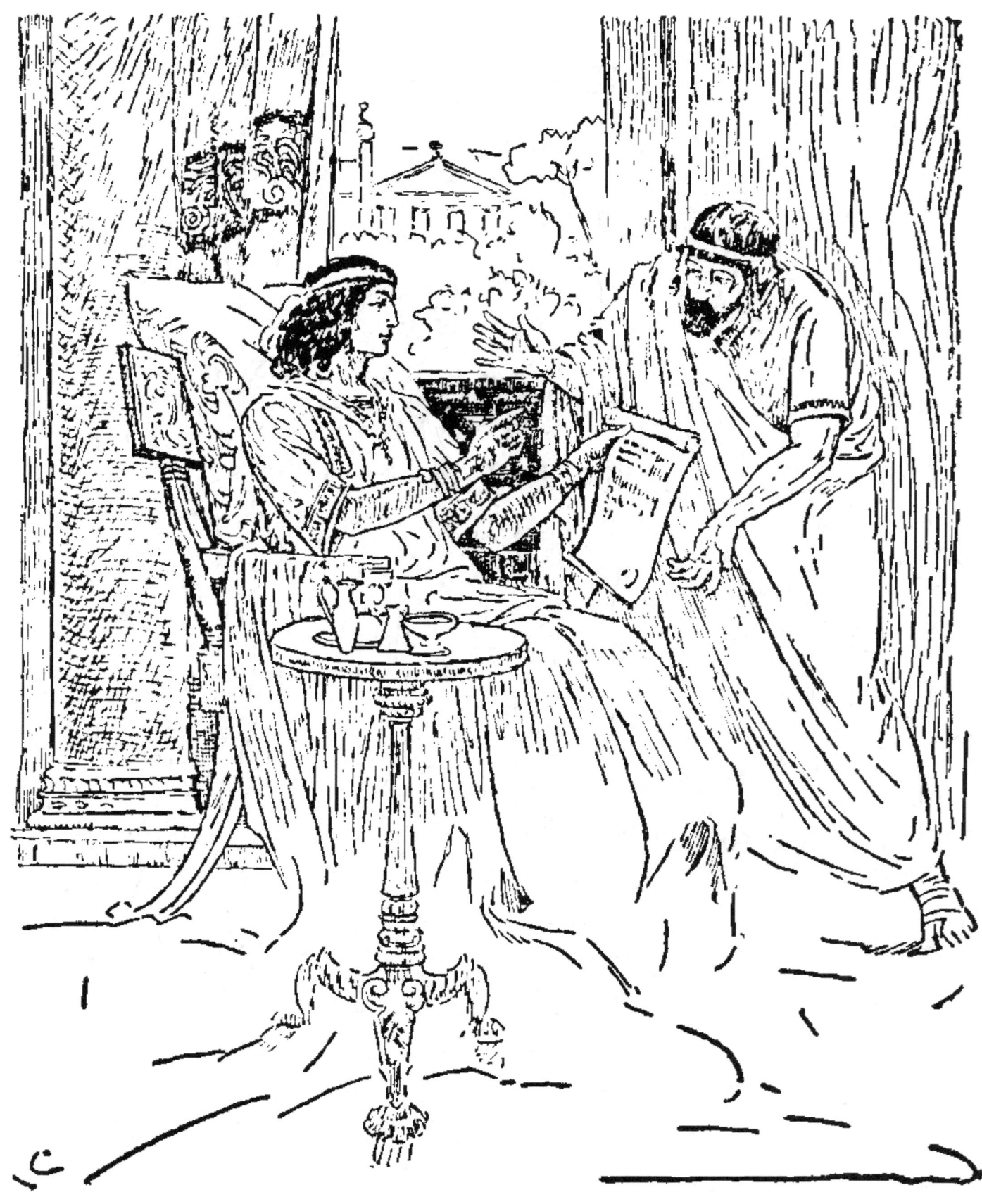

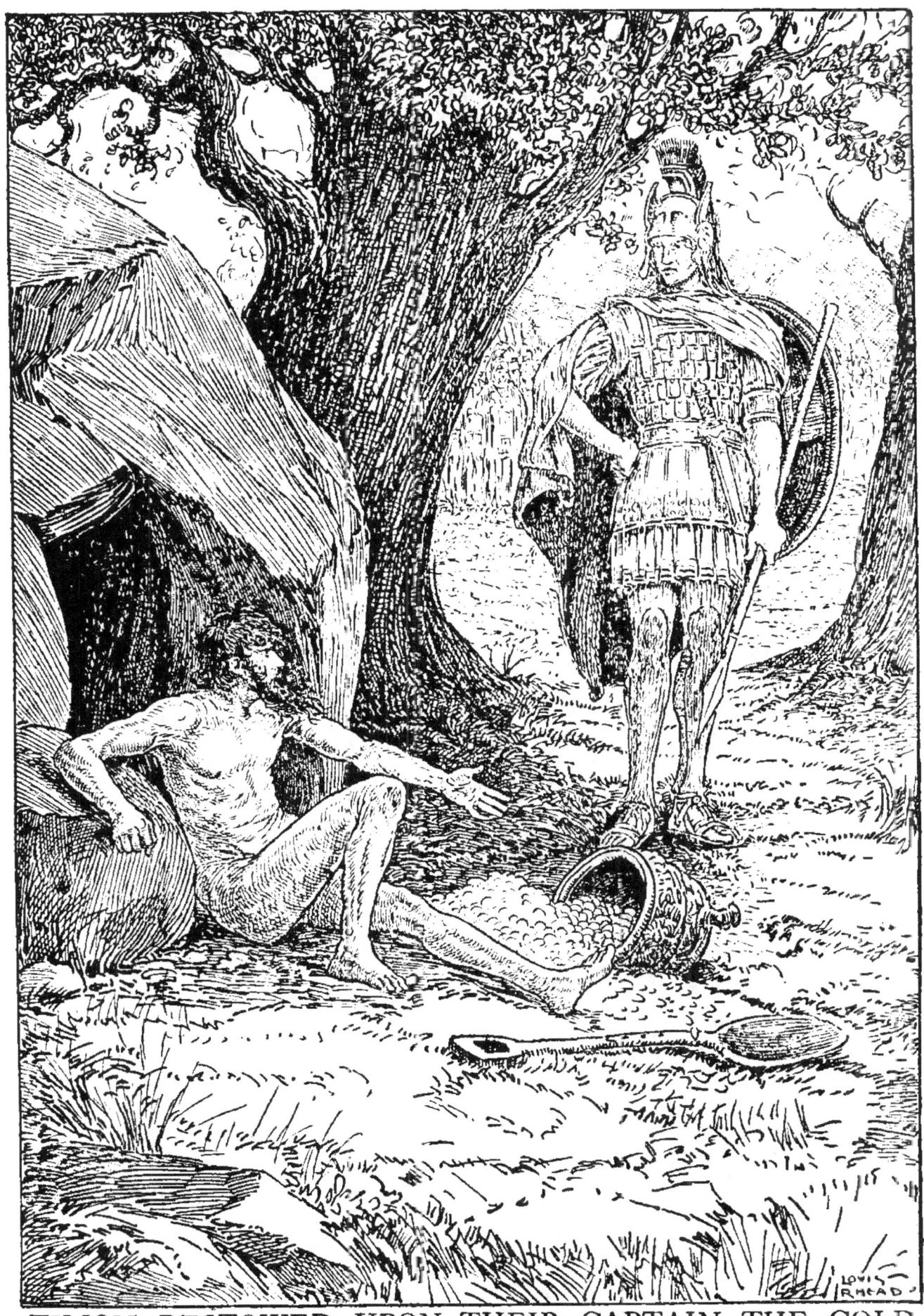

TIMON BESTOWED UPON THEIR CAPTAIN THE GOLD
TO PAY HIS SOLDIERS

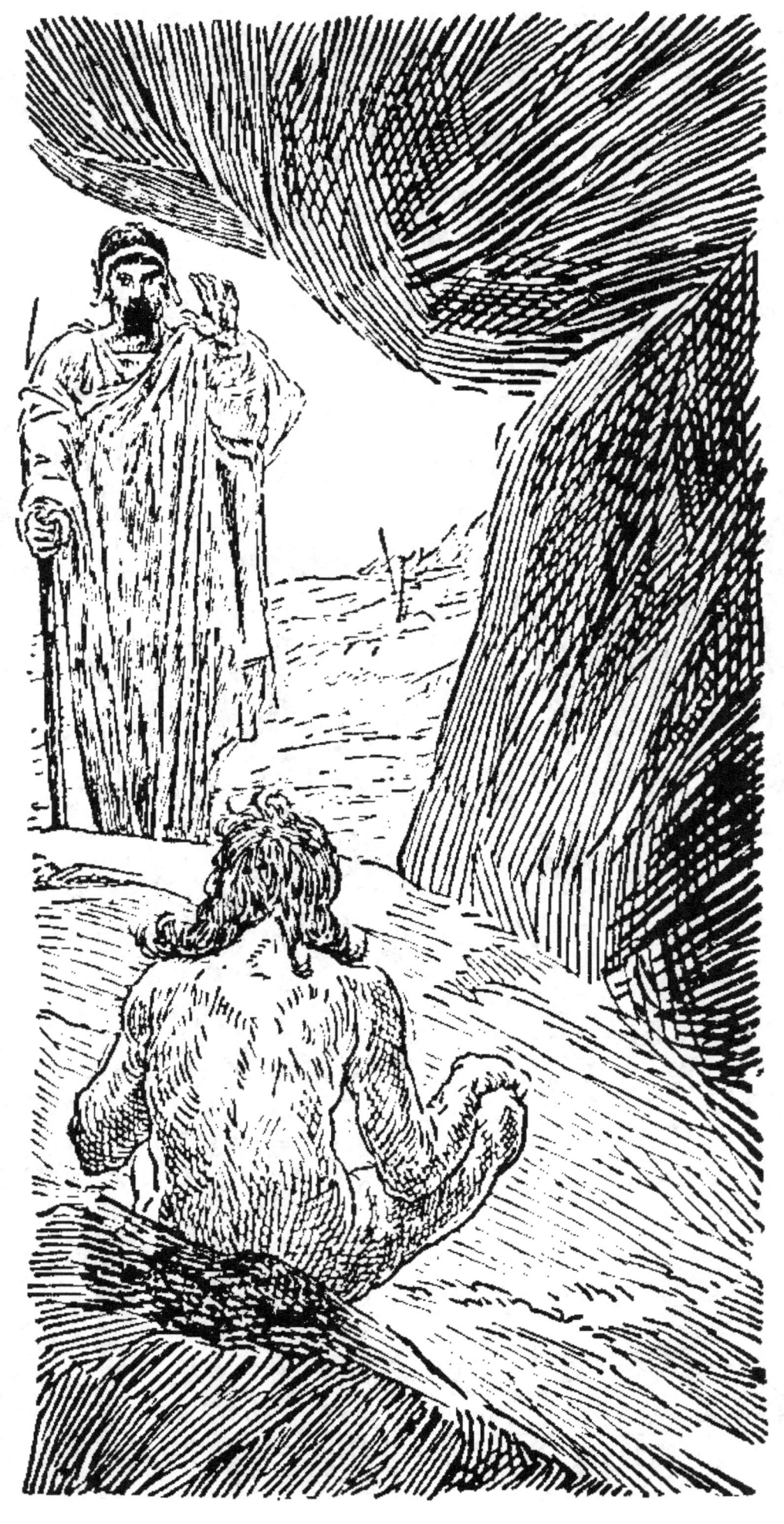

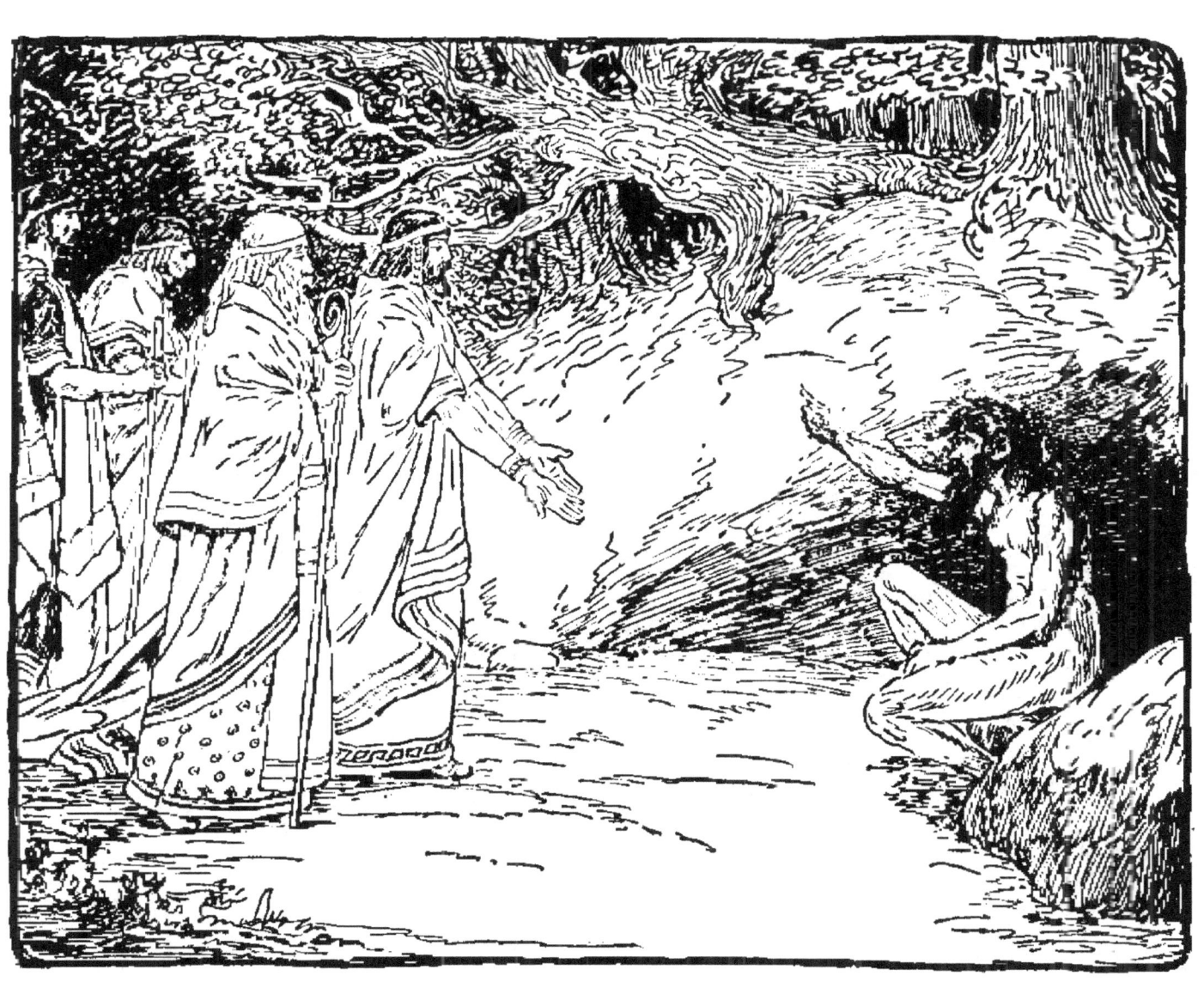

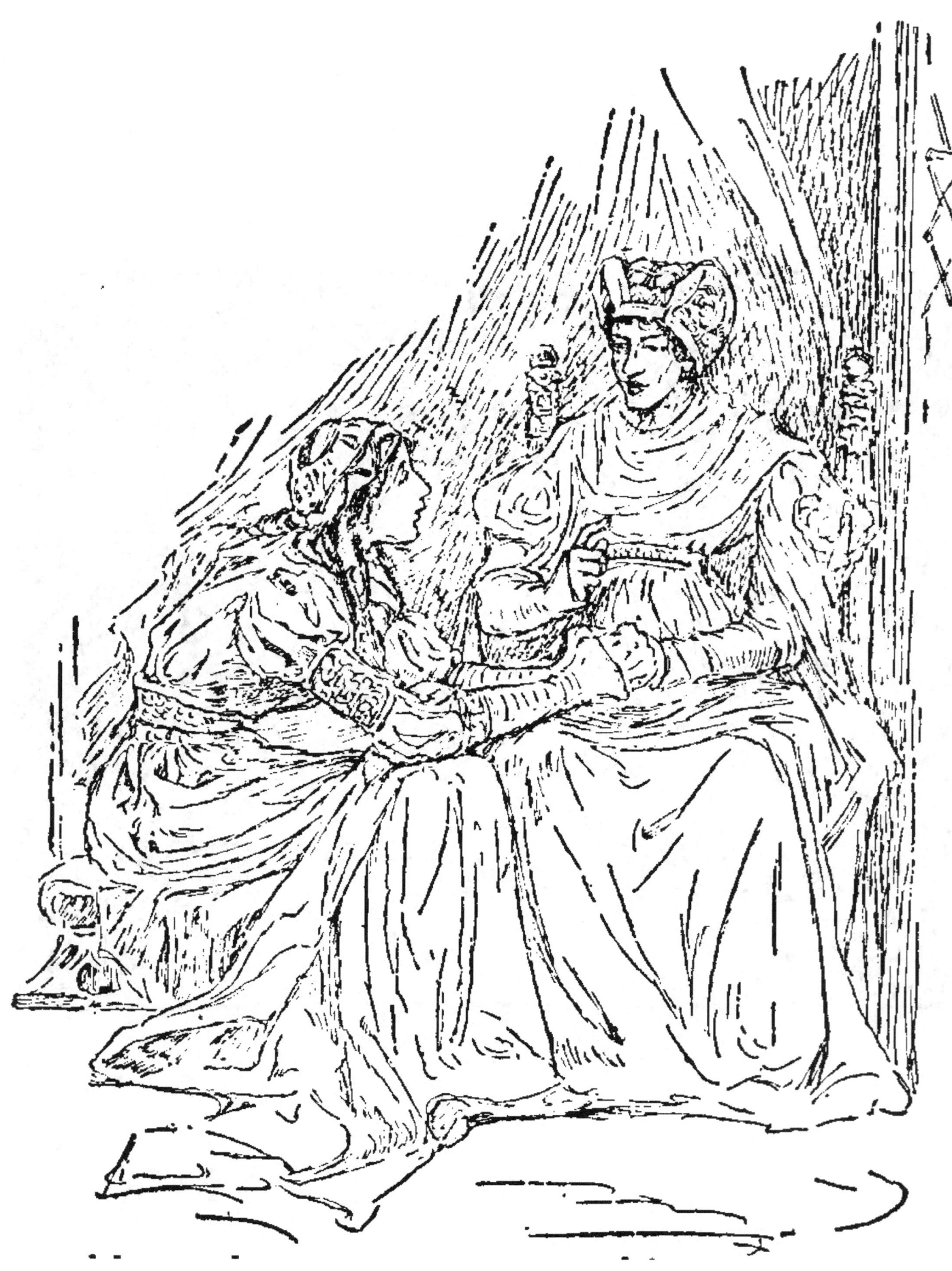

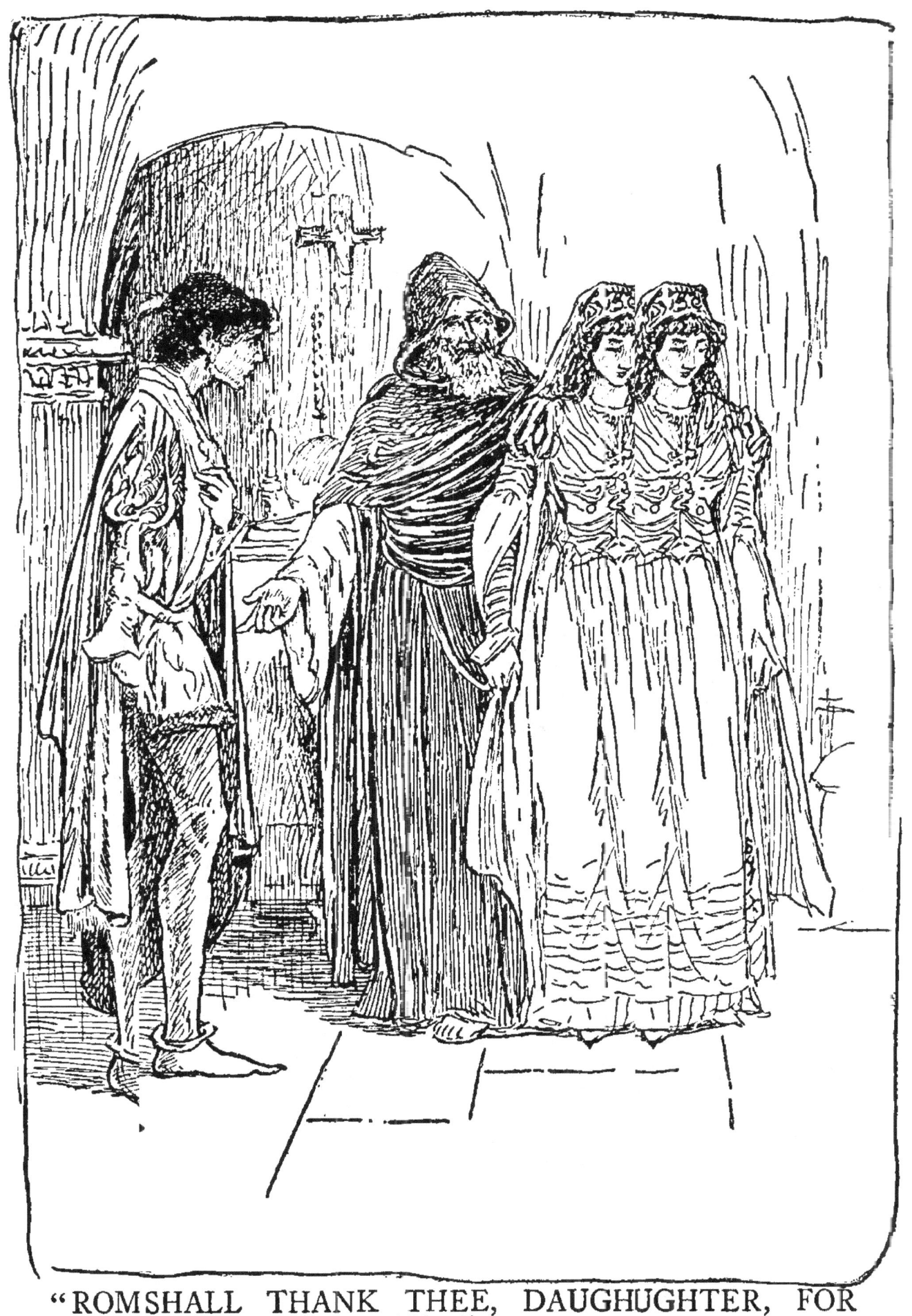

"ROMSHALL THANK THEE, DAUGHUGHTER, FOR US BOTH"

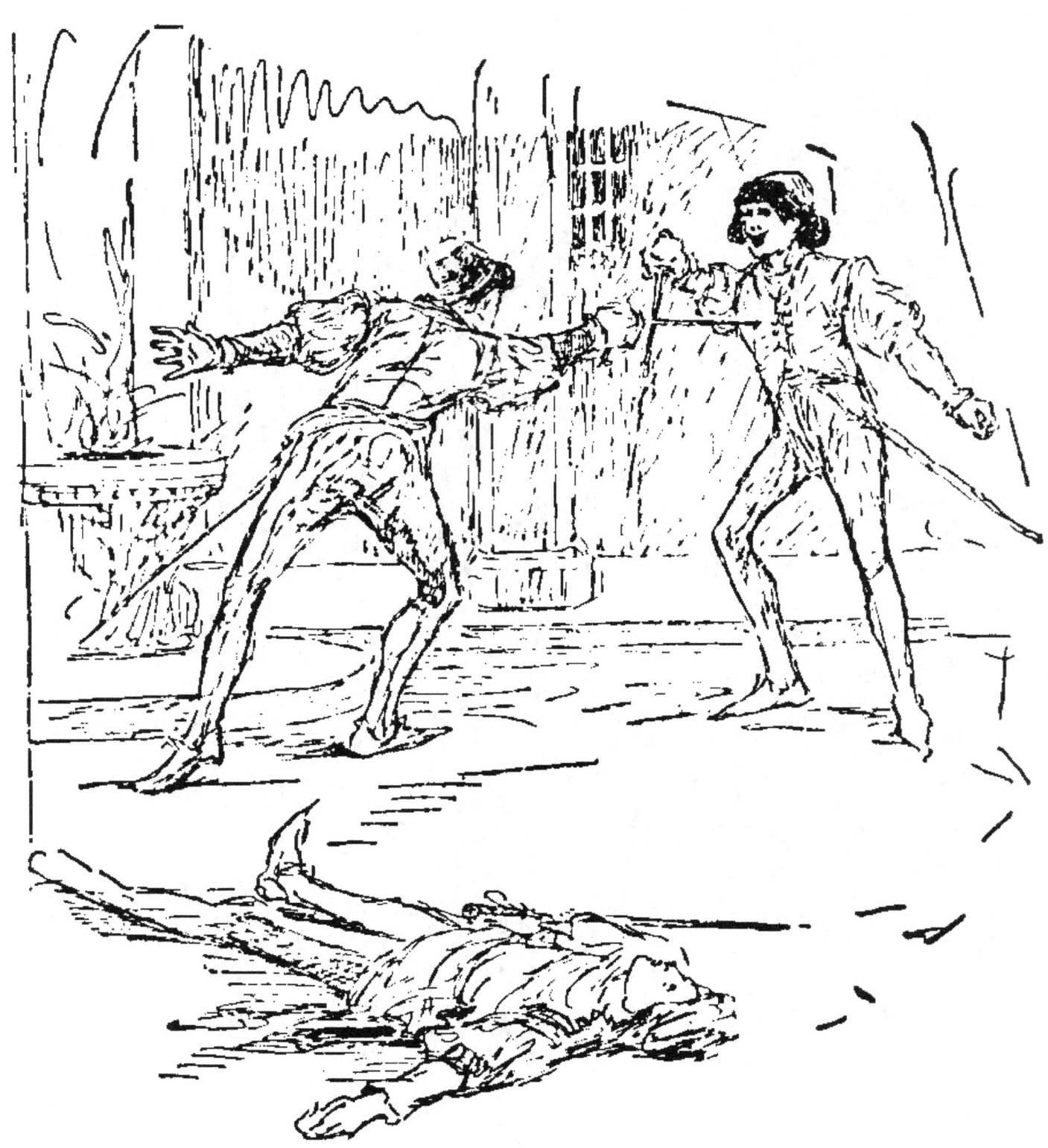

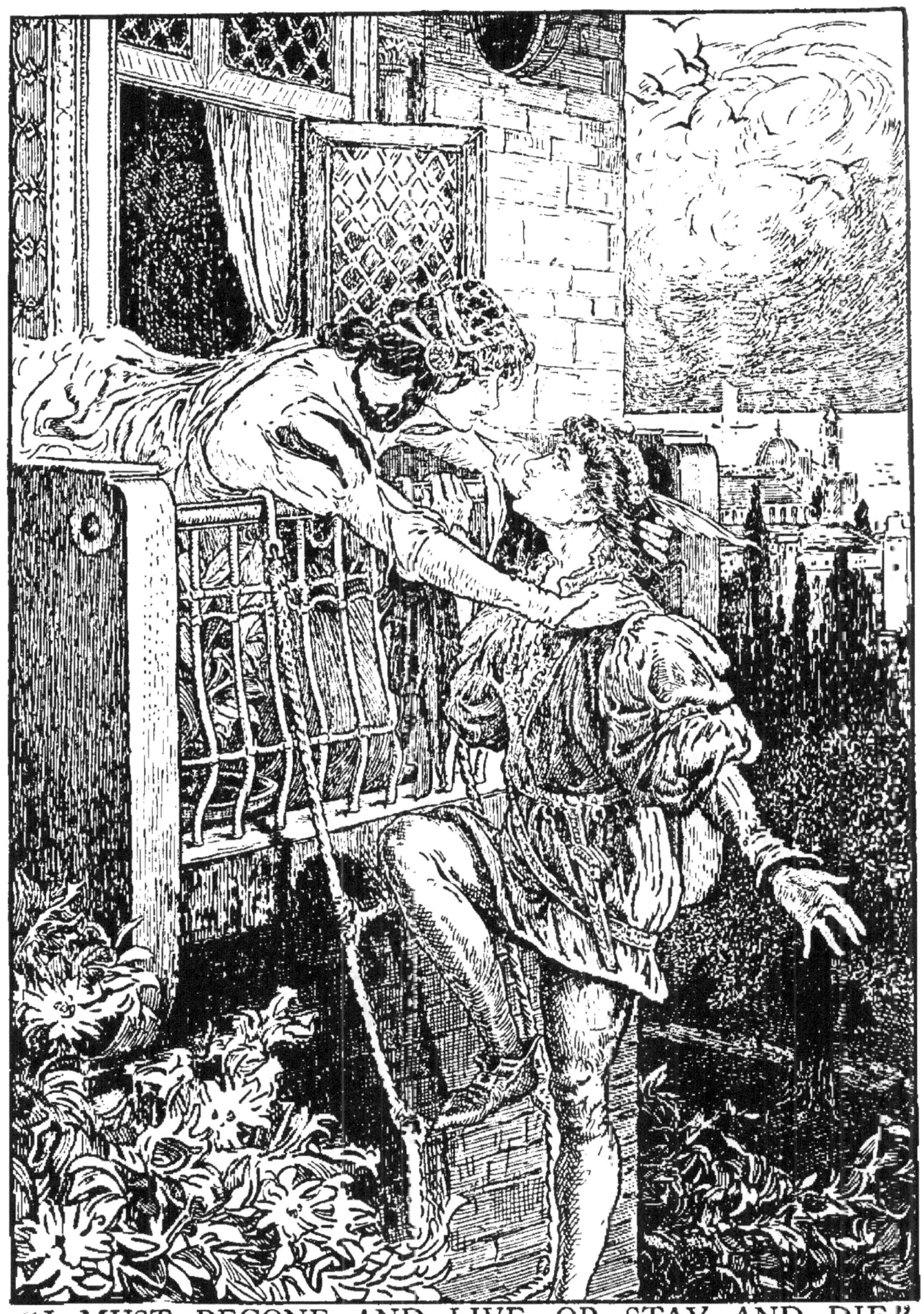

"I MUST BEGONE AND LIVE, OR STAY AND DIE"

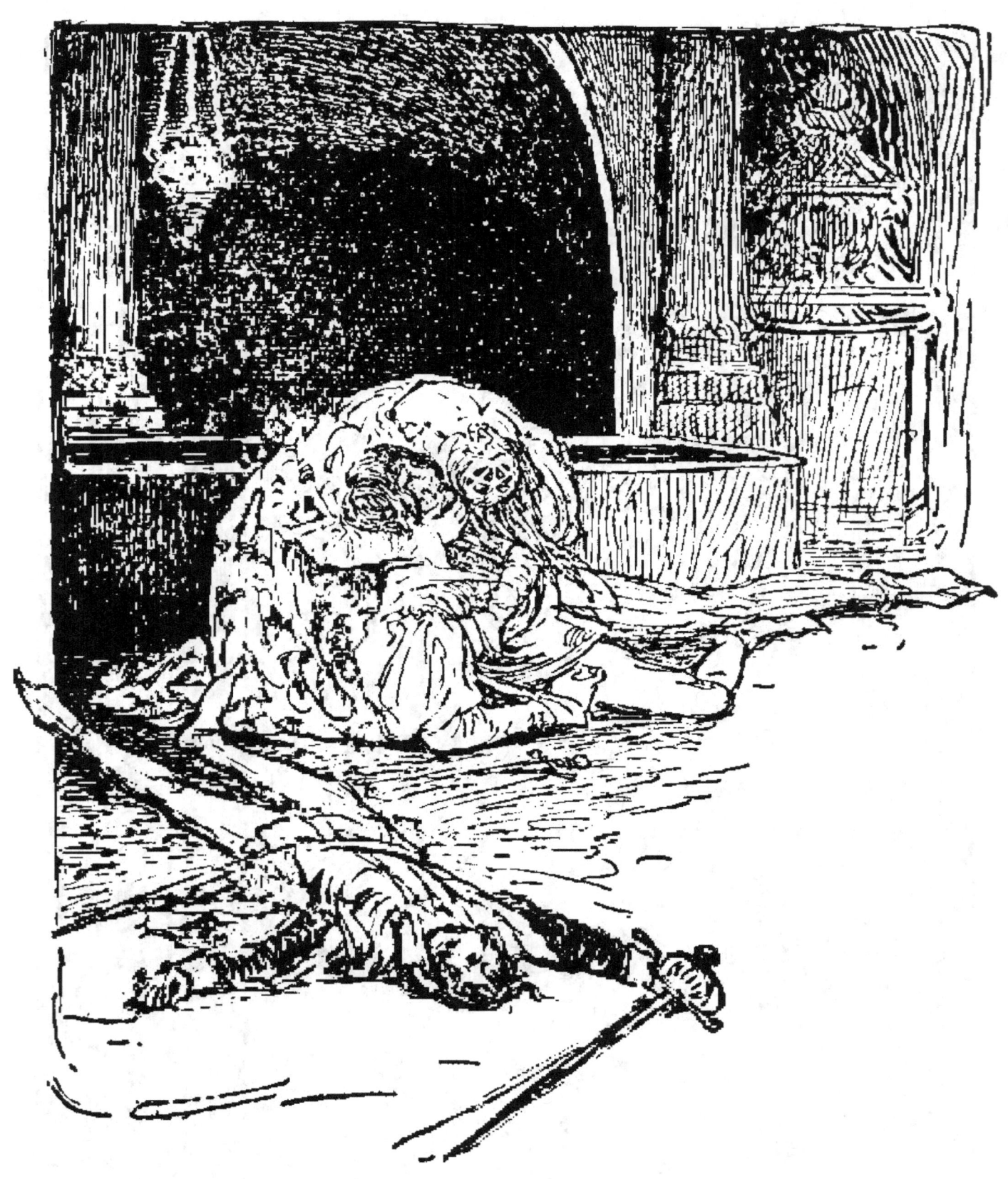

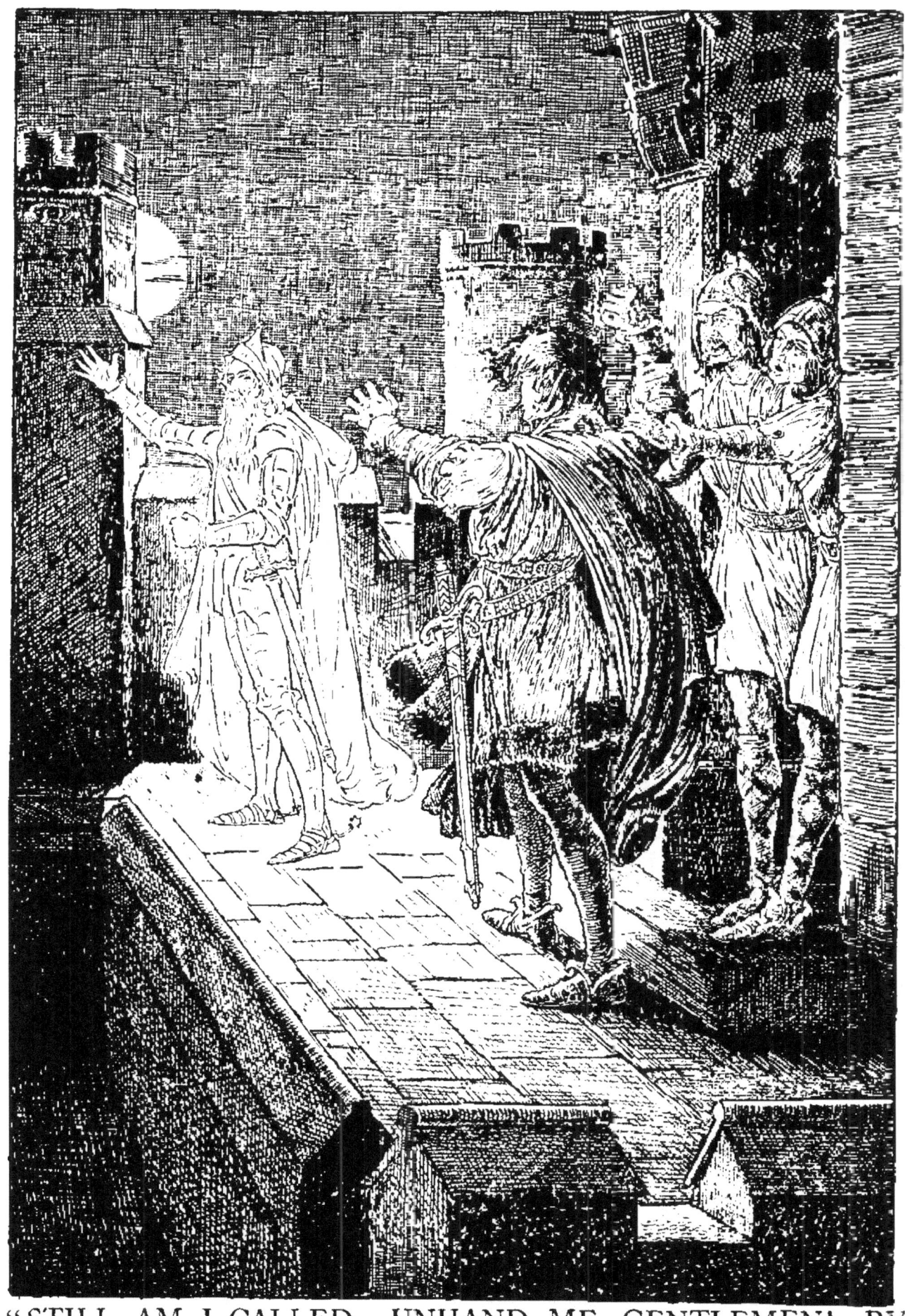

"STILL AM I CALLED. UNHAND ME, GENTLEMEN! BY HEAVEN, I'LL MAKE A GHOST OF HIM THAT LETS ME!"

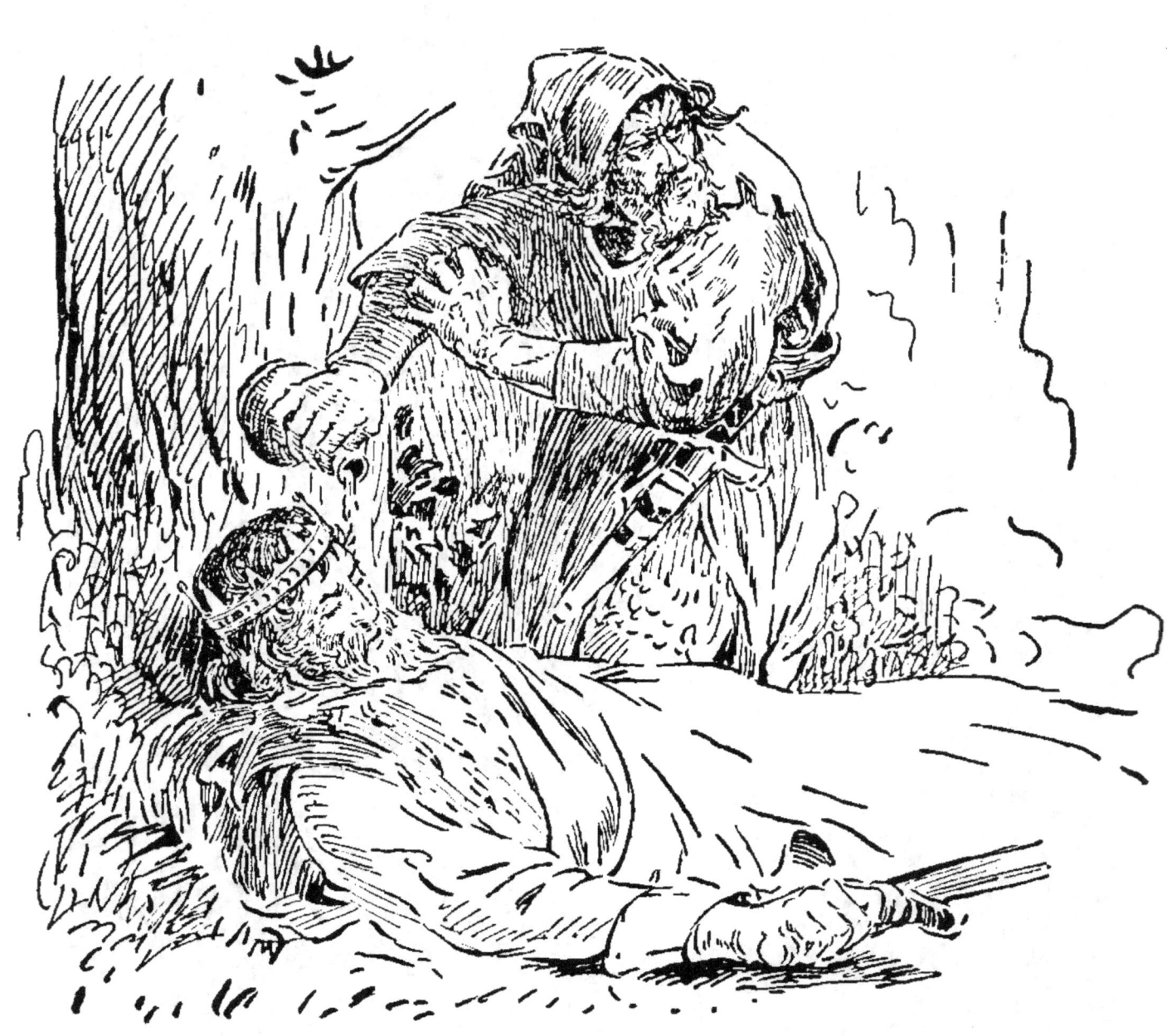

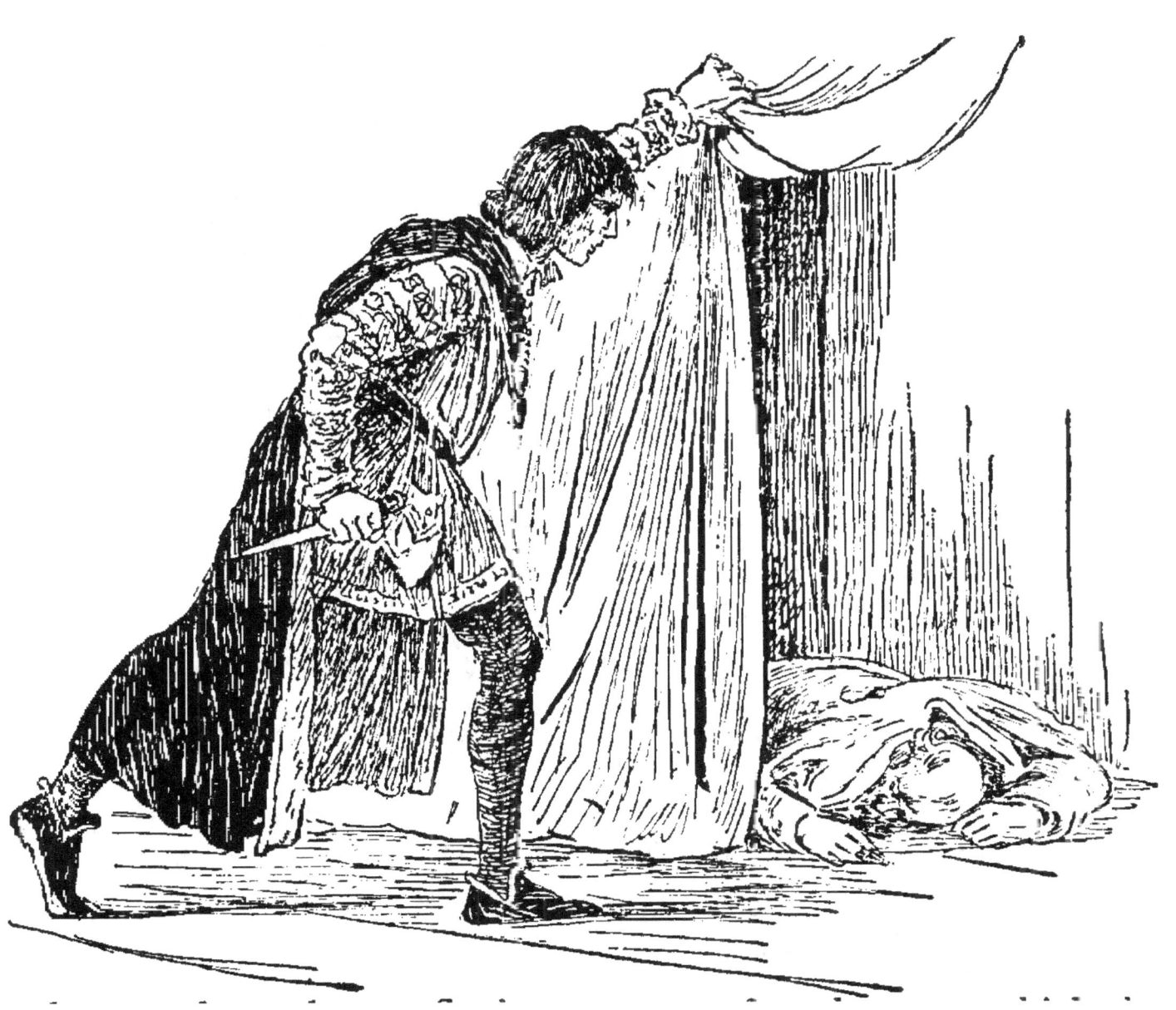

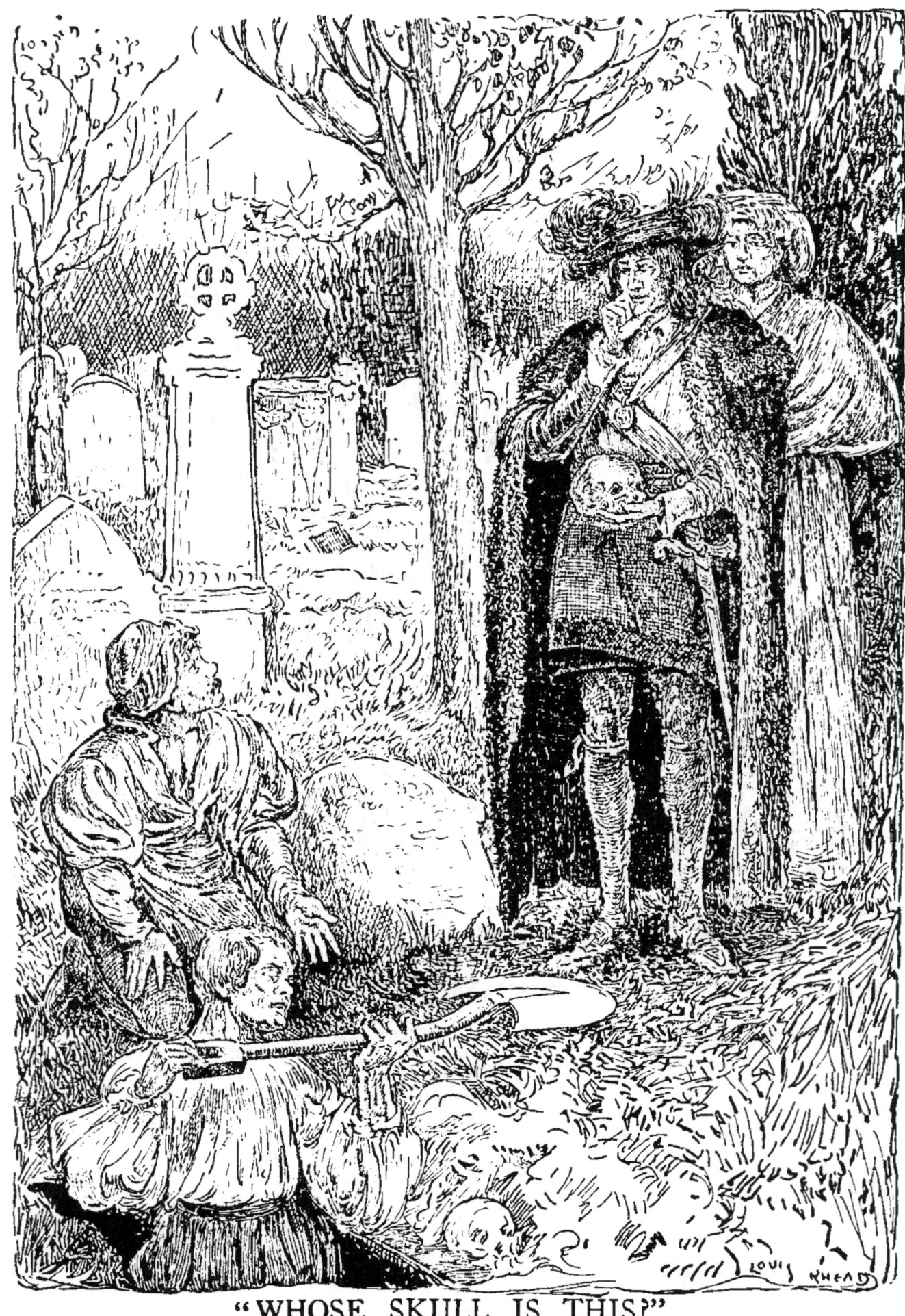

"WHOSE SKULL IS THIS?"

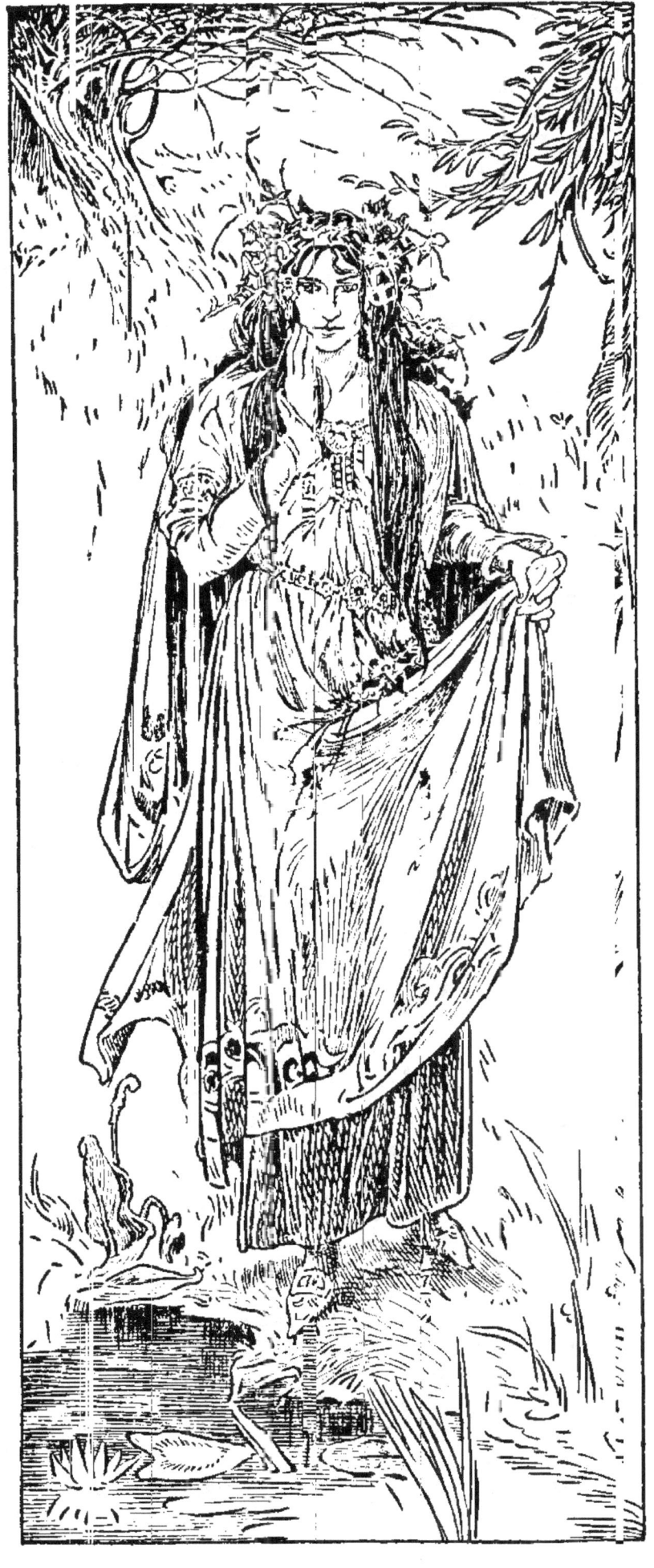

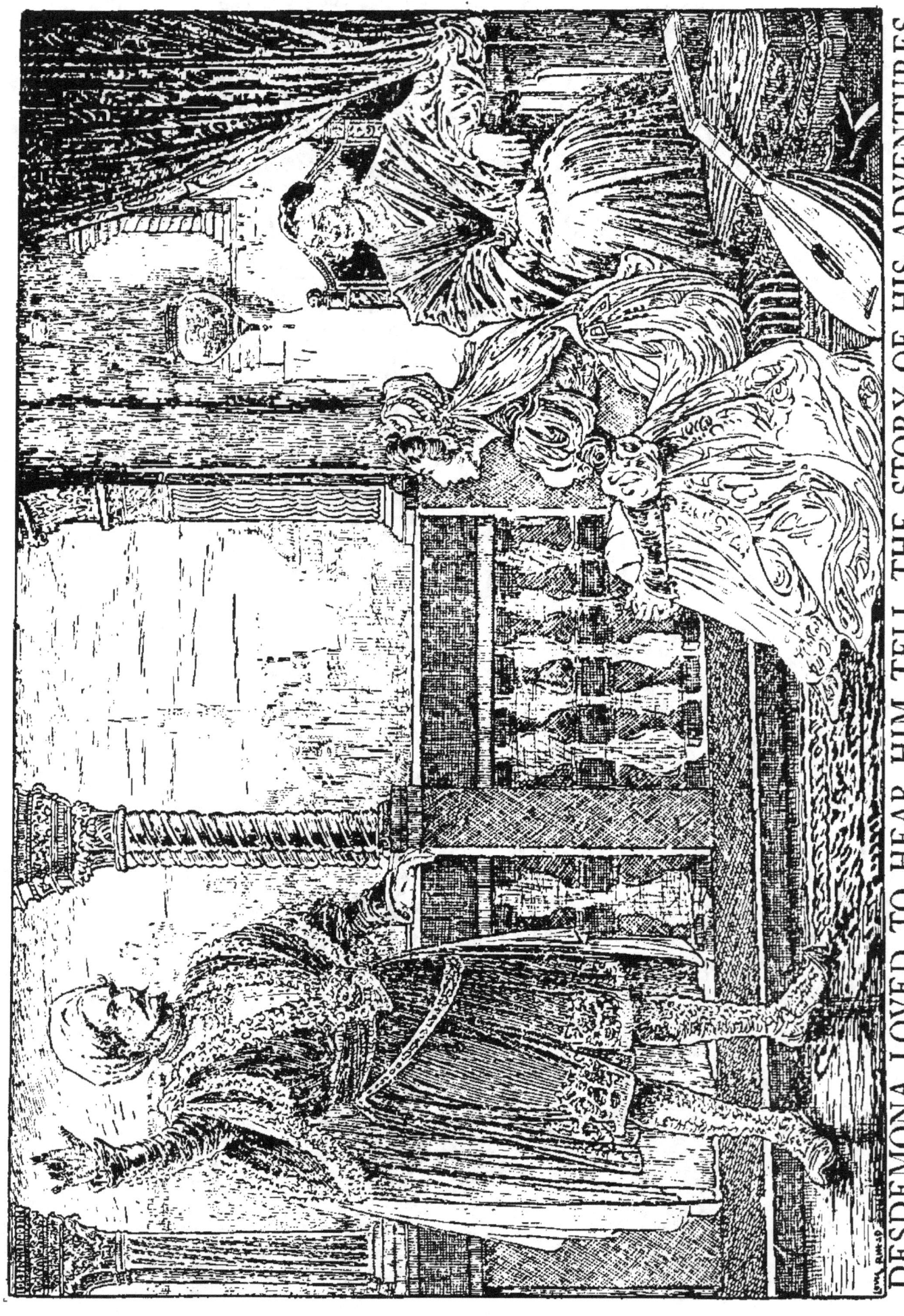

DESDEMONA LOVED TO HEAR HIM TELL THE STORY OF HIS ADVENTURES.

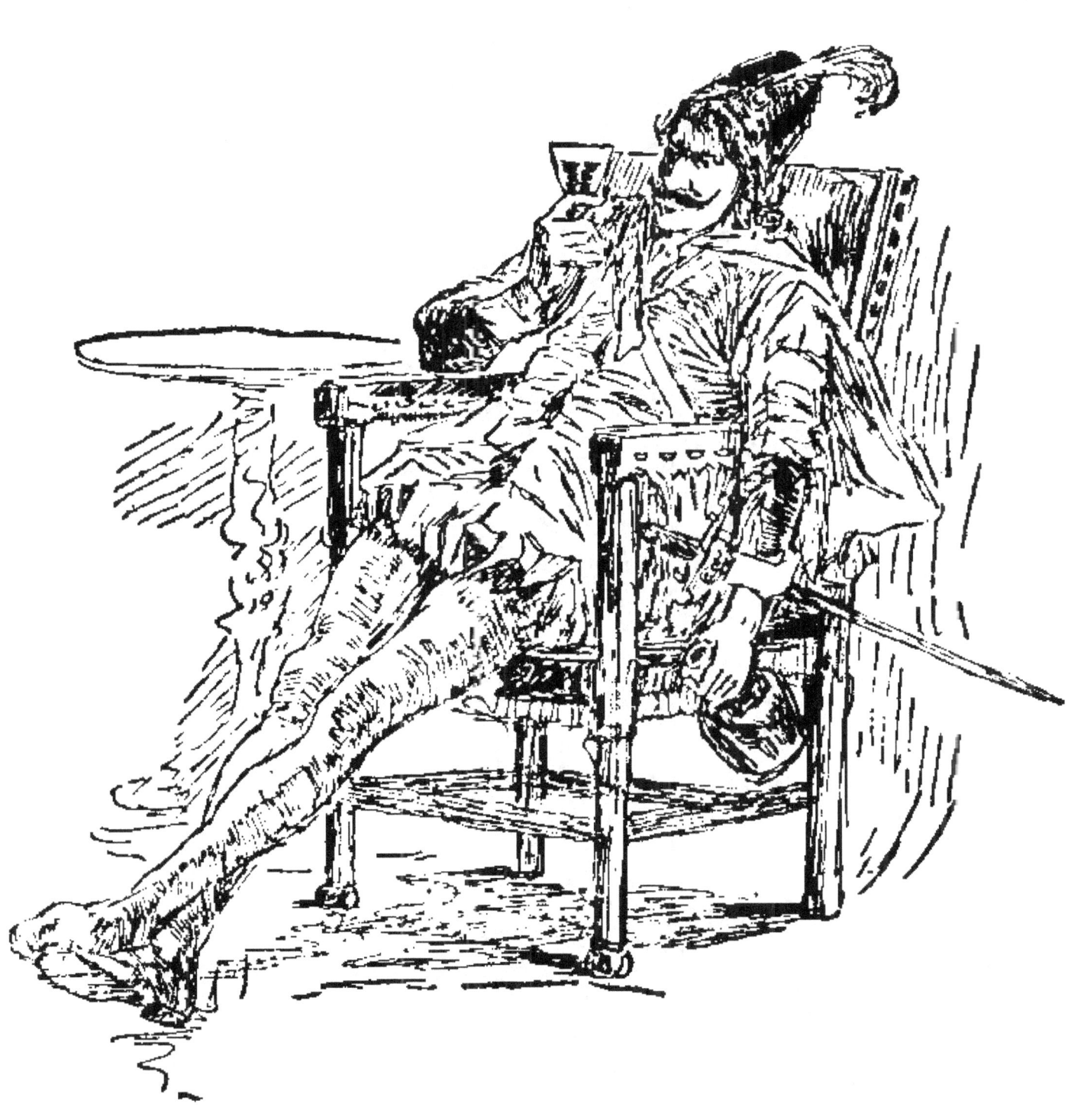

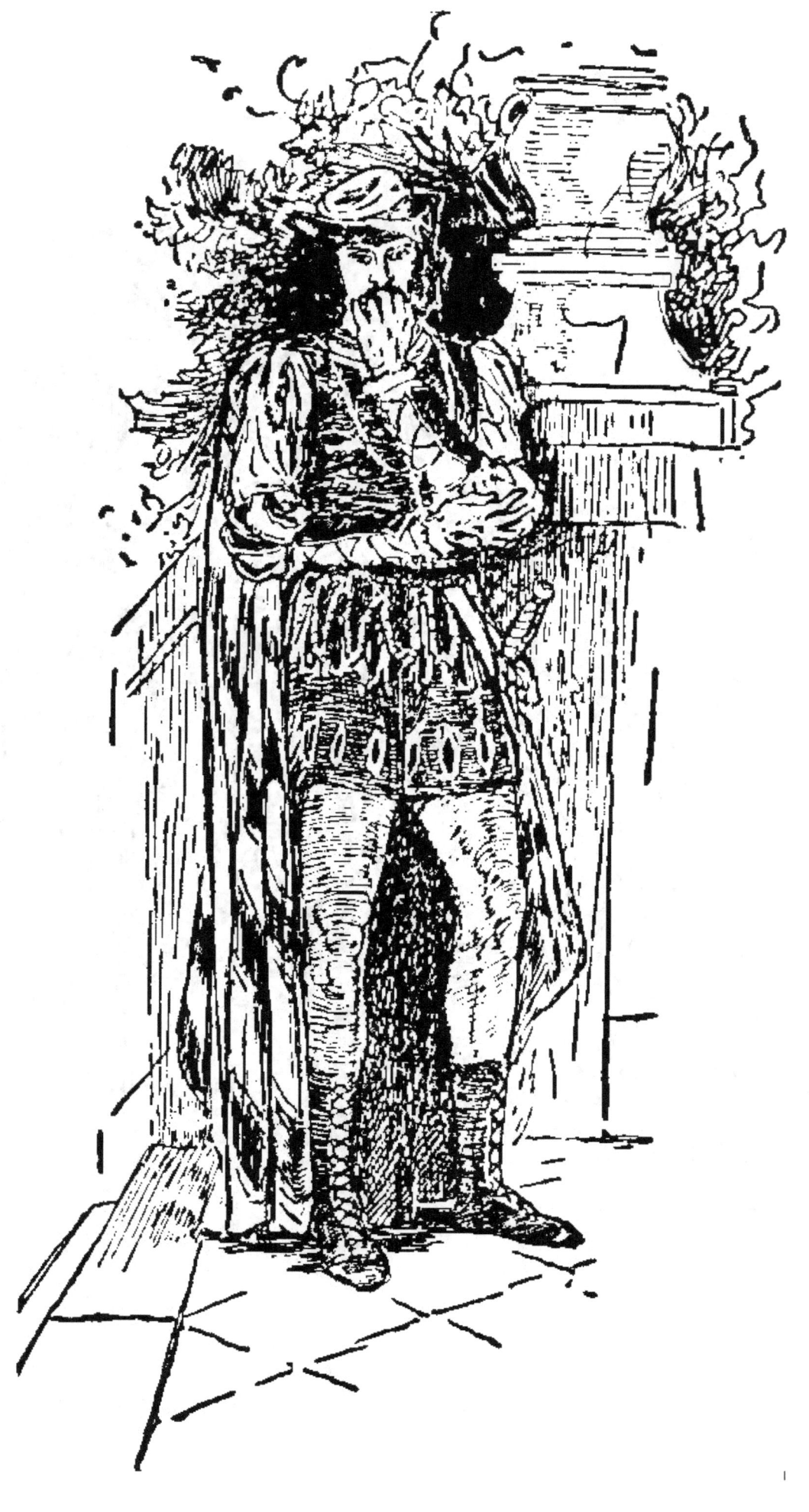

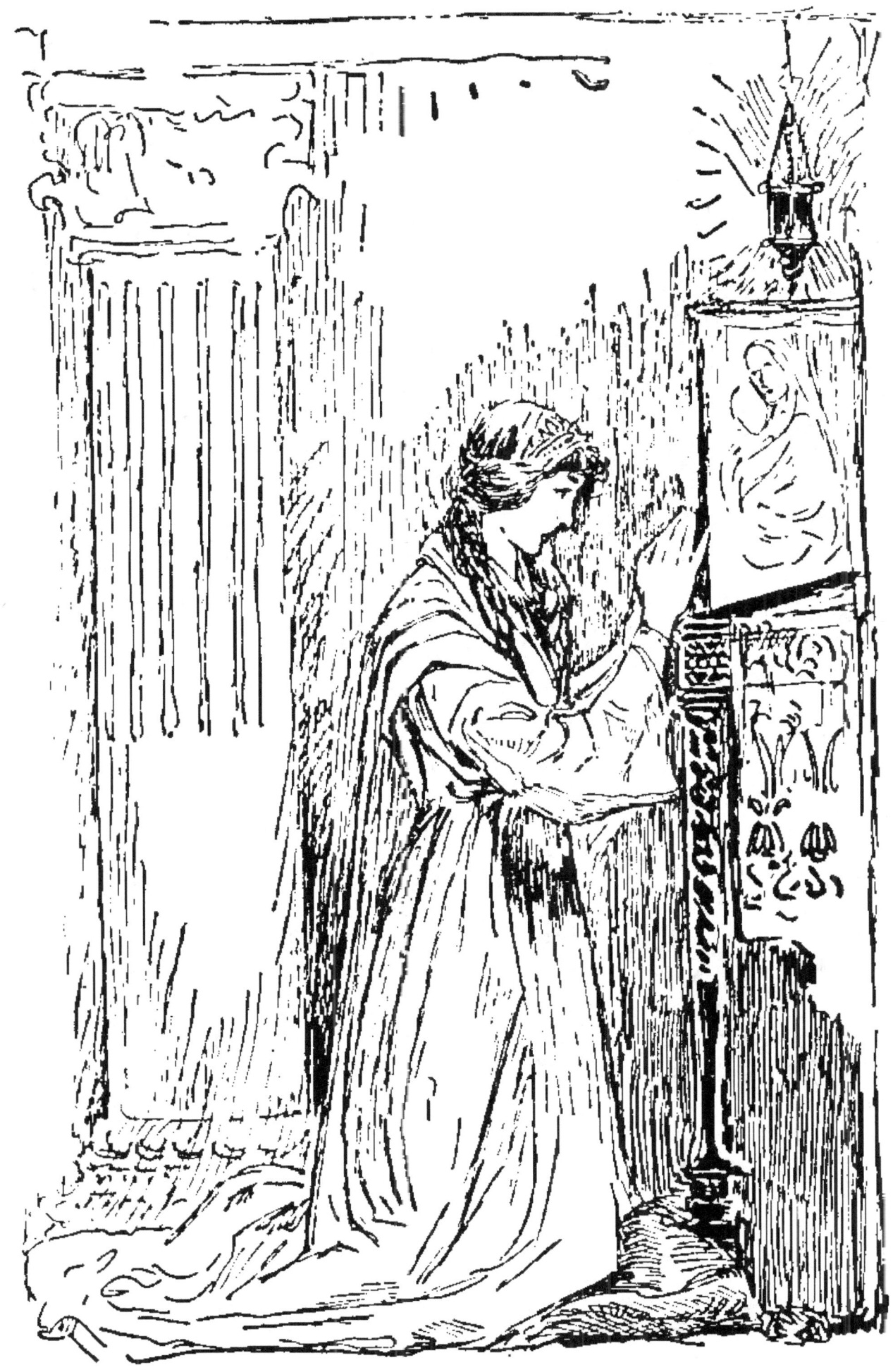

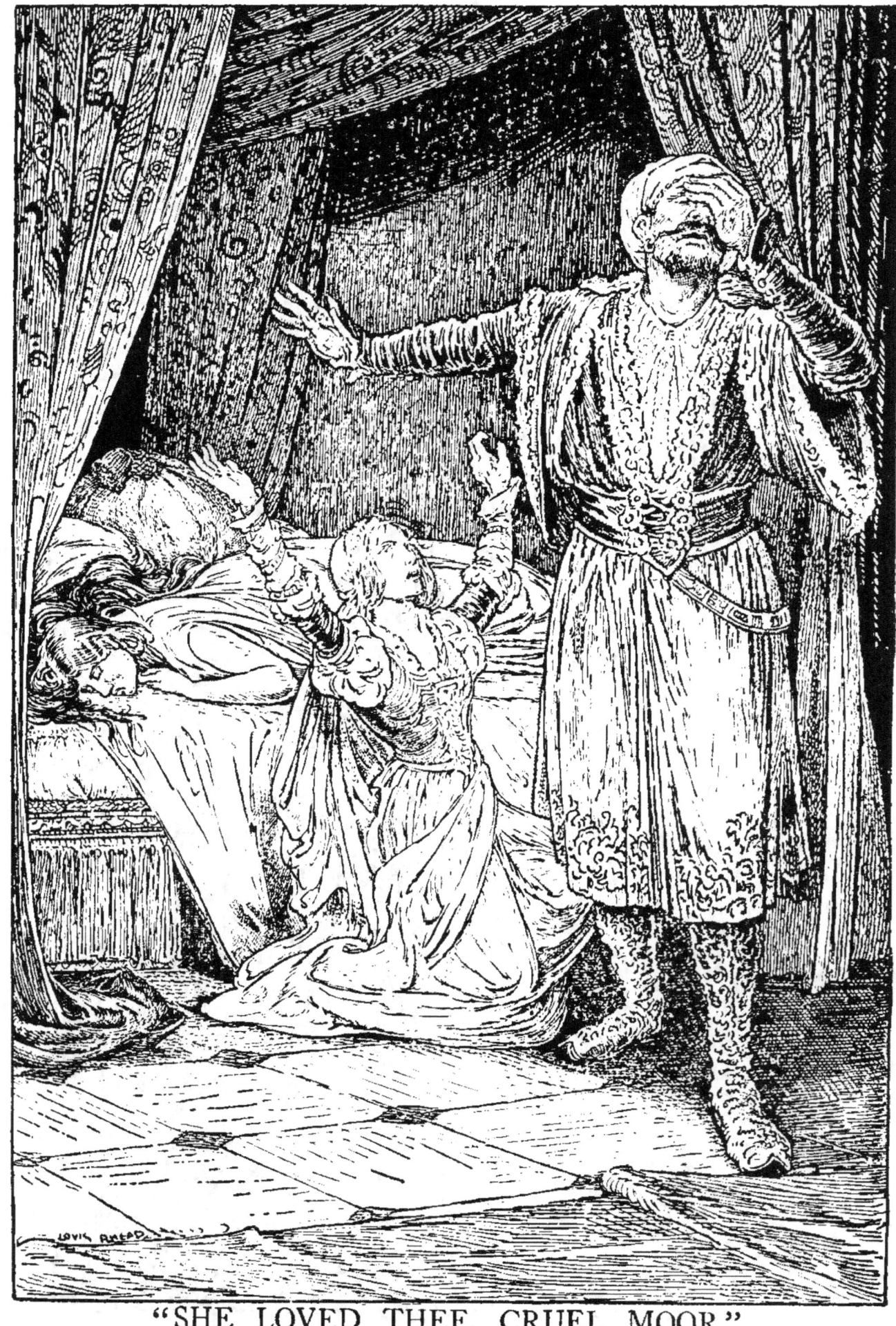
"SHE LOVED THEE, CRUEL MOOR"

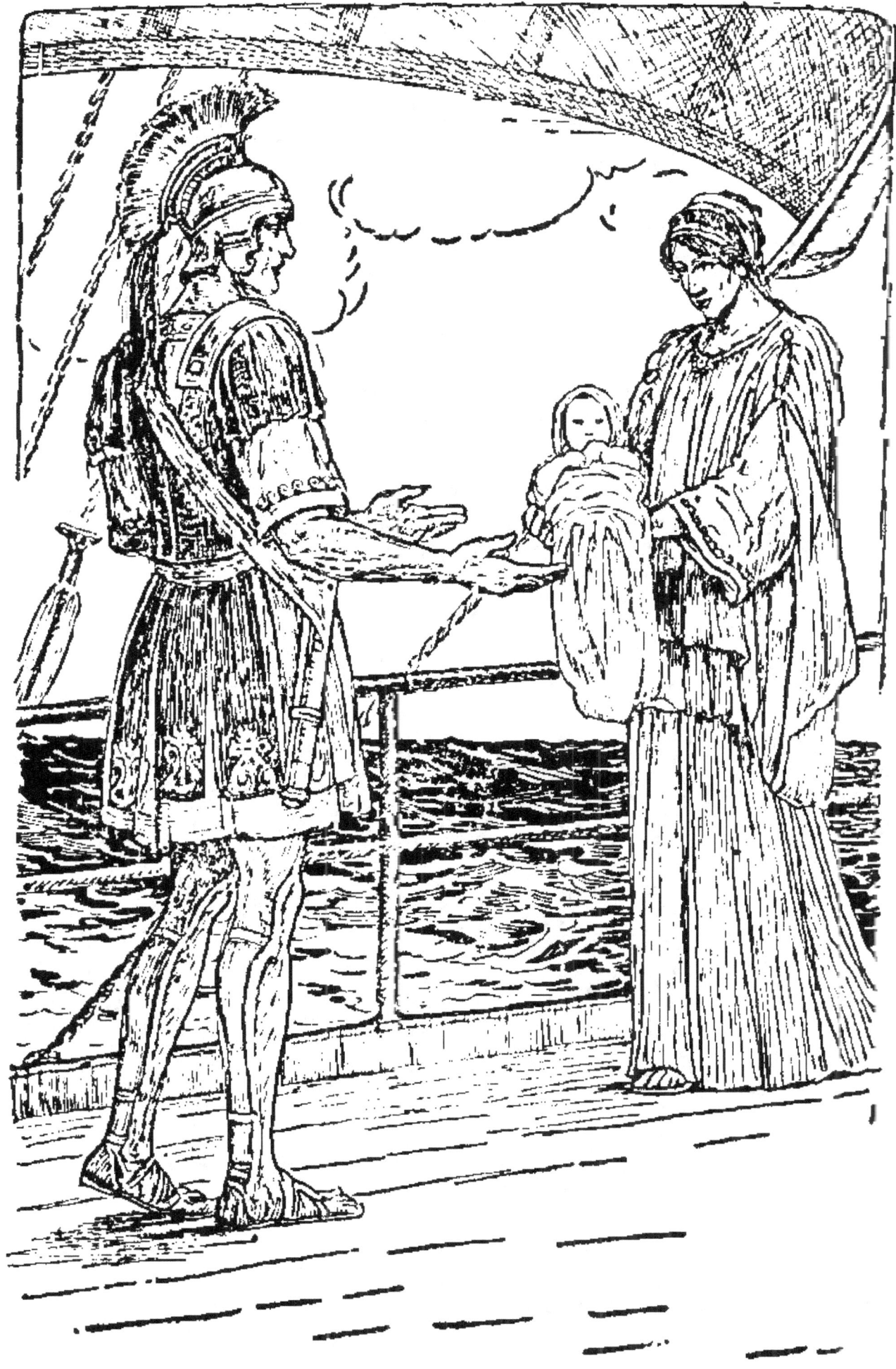

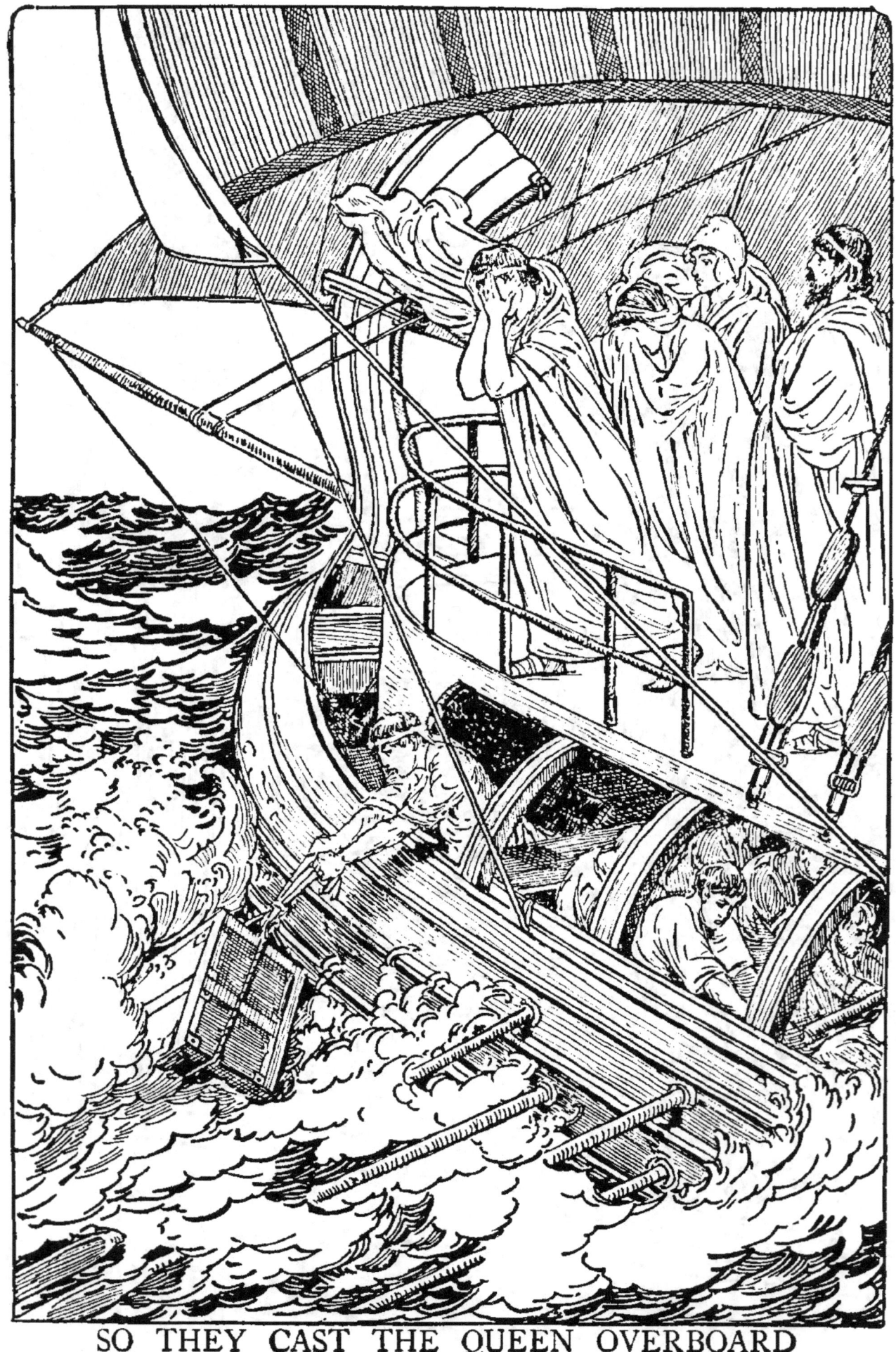
SO THEY CAST THE QUEEN OVERBOARD

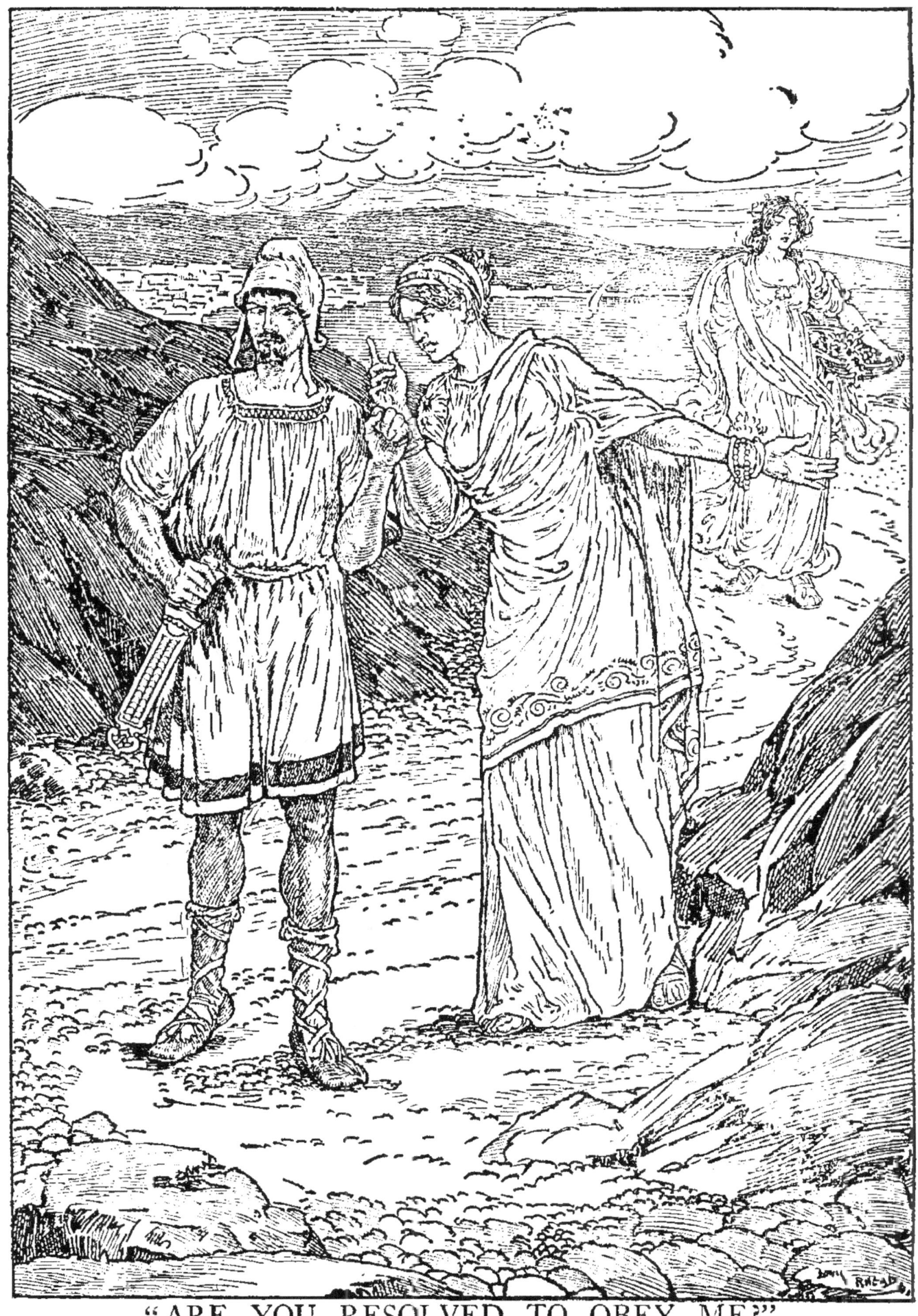
"ARE YOU RESOLVED TO OBEY ME?"

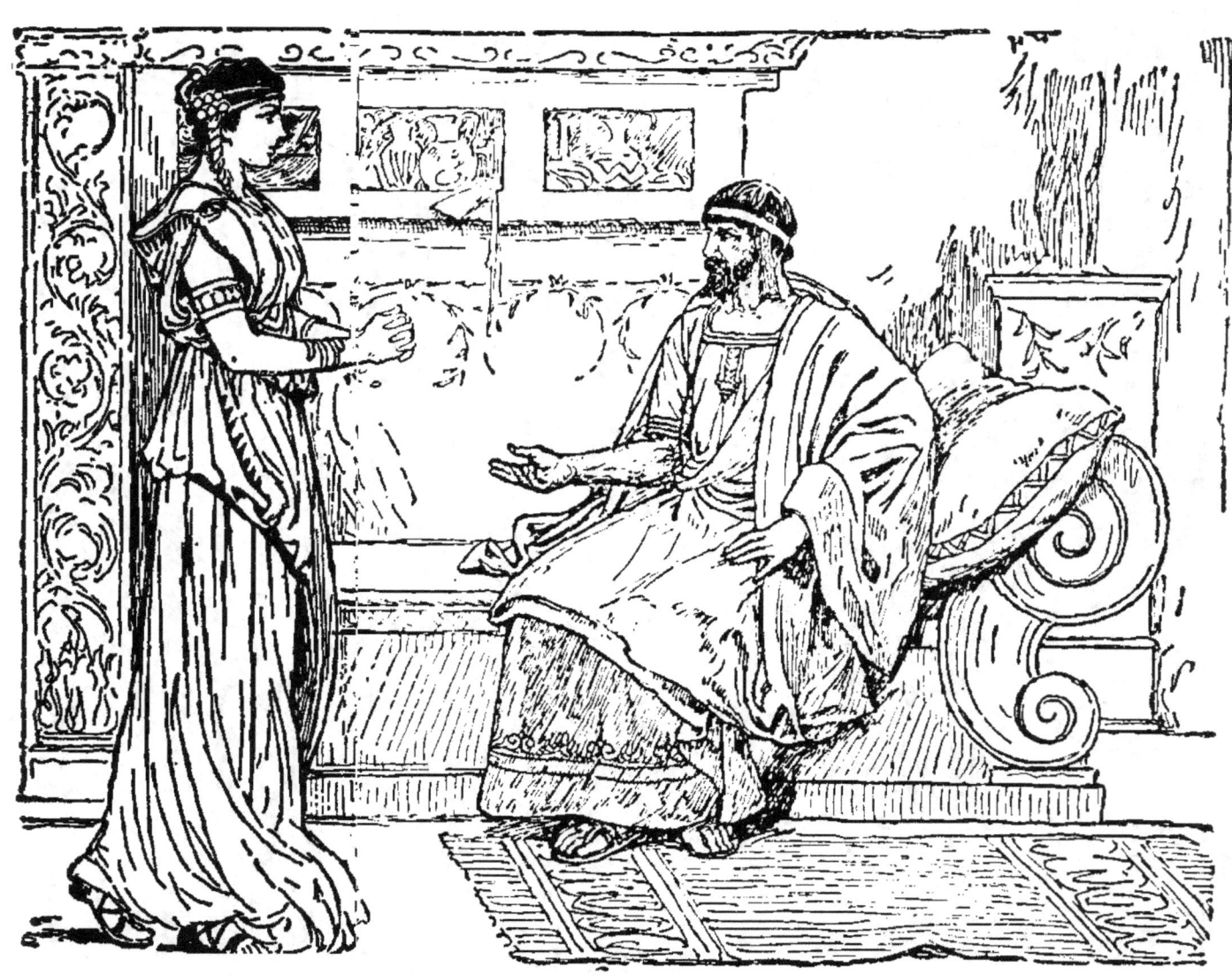

www.ingramcontent.com/pod-product-compliance
Lightning Source LLC
Chambersburg PA
CBHW082116220526
45472CB00009B/2193